BUILDING

ME

BACK

BRICK

BY

BRICK

Thank you for purchasing my book. Your support is greatly appreciated.

Mattie

BUILDING

ME

BACK

BRICK

BY

BRICK

MATTIE LEONARD

gatekeeper press™
Columbus, Ohio

Building Me Back: Brick by Brick

Published by Gatekeeper Press
2167 Stringtown Rd, Suite 109
Columbus, OH 43123-2989
www.GatekeeperPress.com

The cover design, interior formatting, typesetting, and editorial work for this book are entirely the product of the author. Gatekeeper Press did not participate in and is not responsible for any aspect of these elements.

Library of Congress Control Number: 2020946834

ISBN (paperback): 9781662904974
eISBN: 9781662904981

CONTENTS

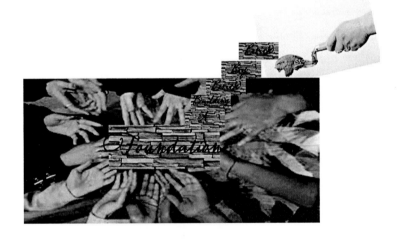

1 Corinthians 3:9

For we are God's fellow workers. You are God's field under cultivation, God's building. (NWT Study Bible)

DEDICATION

Thank you, Lord Jesus, for Building
"Me" Back: Brick by Brick.
To my loving family: daughter Shanetta, granddaughter
A'Lisa, mother Maria, father Raymond, and
close friend James, who have all supported me
throughout my battle with addiction and have
been a supportive force in my life. Without them, I
would not have made it to a successful recovery.
Thank you so much. I love each and
every one of you. KISSES.

INTRODUCTION

Thank you for taking the time to read my book and listen to my story. Your support is greatly appreciated. If you let it, this book will change your perspective on life. From visiting crack houses to my many other quests to retrieve drugs, I found myself in several compromising situations. *Building "Me" Back: Brick by Brick* brings awareness to addiction through my own life experiences and has been written to help others in their recovery process. Relapse was a part of my story, but it does not have to be a part of yours. This memoir shows how, through external pressures and self-induced internal pressures, my foundation had been broken and needed to be rebuilt. It wasn't an easy task.

"Life on life's terms" happens, and I learned that you have to go through the struggles instead of hiding behind drugs, pills, alcohol, and sex. *Building "Me" Back: Brick by Brick* is the story of me creating a deep crack in my foundation through the trials of life — the abstinence from drug use I never wanted to have. In rebuilding one brick at a time, I found out that the crack in my foundation could be traced back to my childhood past, long before I ever decided to pick up the first drug. I make it clear that my attraction to drugs cost me so many things: my car, my money, and nearly my house and my life. I hope that my story will show you mentally, physically, spiritually, and emotionally how to deal and how *not* to deal with your addiction. I will explain how stressors are a part of life that must be dealt with head-on and not run from. I've learned firsthand about addiction, having worked through the fight of getting clean from various mood-altering substances. These included street drugs, in addition to prescribed medication and alcohol. I want to help other addicts who struggle and feel like recovery is not possible. Your recovery is your responsibility, and it takes a dedicated effort to be successful.

Writing *Building "Me" Back: Brick by Brick* has helped me define the addictive behavior in my own life, pinpoint when the disease of addiction first manifested, and learn how to press through the obstacles that contributed to my use. The earlier you pinpoint when your addiction started, the better equipped you are to heal through recovery. Through the lens of my own story of addiction, I will show that addiction is the product of character defects that can span a lifetime of work to heal. But it can be accomplished through the twelve steps of the Narcotics Anonymous program. As the bricklayer needs a trowel and mortar, so an addict needs new tools to build their foundation all over again. These tools include spiritual principles, sponsorship, and listening to other members' life experiences and hopes at Narcotics Anonymous meetings. What has also helped me in my recovery is undergoing a type of psychotherapy in which negative patterns of thought about the self and the world are challenged in order to alter unwanted behavior patterns or to treat mood disorders such as depression and anxiety.

I ultimately realized that God allowed the stressors in my life to bless me and to reveal my weaknesses. I am grateful for the pressures that have pressed me closer to Him and caused me to allow God to be my strength. Through a realization down deep in my soul that my life has purpose, I pray that I can provide a powerful dynamic for blessing the lives of others.

PART 1

Before My Active Addiction

A bricklayer is a skilled member of a trade who constructs brickwork. He uses a trowel and mortar, the superglue of masonry, to hold the work together. Plan the foundation of your structure, using the metaphor of a bricklayer laying down brick from start to finish. Without a solid foundation, over time the elements of life will cause cracks to form in your structure. Restoring or avoiding cracks is all about having a system in place to make your life better. It's rewarding to see the results of your work with your own two hands, building a wall or a building of some sort. The bottom line is, you have to plan the work of recovery and work the plan.

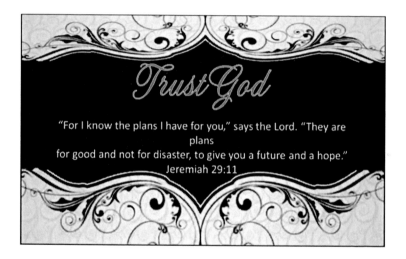

Trust God

"For I know the plans I have for you," says the Lord. "They are plans
for good and not for disaster, to give you a future and a hope."
Jeremiah 29:11

CHAPTER ONE

··

STRUGGLING WITH SUICIDAL THOUGHTS

Did you know?

According to the Centers for Disease Control (CDC) and the World Health Organization (WHO), suicide is the second-leading cause of death in the world for people ages 10 to 34. Each year, approximately one million people die from suicide, and this represents a global mortality rate of one death by suicide every forty seconds. It is predicted that by 2020, the rate of death will increase to one every twenty seconds, with females being more likely than males to have suicidal thoughts (SAVE, 2020).

I consider my parents as the craftsmen in the construction of the foundation to my brickwork and God as the trowel in my life. Thus, the first layer of my brickwork was developed through my parents. I was born to a petite lady from Panama, in Harlem Hospital, in Manhattan, New York. The man that impregnated my mother wanted nothing to do with me and vanished from our life. My mom, being a strong lady, did what was best for me and her and went on with her life. She raised me as a single parent until she met a native North Carolina man, who was in the Coast Guard, one day at my aunt Nora's house in New York. He would come by there to visit on a regular basis. He would play with me all the time, because I would run to him whenever he came. We hit it off way before my mother met him. He adored me, and questioned who was the mother of this child. He was determined to meet my mother. When they finally met, they were head over heels for each other. After dating a few months, they decided to get married, and he adopted me as his own. Finally, I had a man I could call my dad. We moved to Goldsboro, North Carolina, when he decided to get out of the Coast Guard. I recall us living in a brown trailer with a swing set outside, surrounded by pink-flowered trees. The swing set consisted of a single swing, a face-to-face swing, and a tandem swing seat. The face-to-face swing was my favorite. It was suitable for two children at the same time. I loved that swing set and used to fall asleep swinging on the face-to-face swing all the time. We lived there for several years before my dad decided to join the Army. Once in the Army, he got orders to go to Germany. We went with him and moved as a family to Giessen, Germany. I used to take long nature walks on the trails that were near my house. One day my friends and I stole some cigarettes from my dad, and we were experimenting with them on a bench that was along the trail. I nearly choked, and from that day decided that smoking wasn't for me. I was a very happy child, having a mom and a dad. My life was now on a solid foundation until we moved to Texas. Little did I know my dad had been having many extramarital affairs that were causing the breakdown of the marriage, not to mention the hotheadedness of my

Panamanian mother. She threatened to leave him as soon as we got back to the States. The lack of trust in people was now developing in my life, thus creating a crack in my so-called solid foundation.

Growing up Through my Teen Years

DAD

My dad spent quality time with me in my younger years. He spent more time with me as a child than my mother did, talking and playing cards and games. He was the fun and outgoing parent, so it was inevitable that I would have a void when my father left. I can count on one hand the number of times he ever raised his voice at me. He never spanked me—that was my mom's job.

My father was a soldier in the Army. I recall one time when he came home, he had a sponge cut in the shape of a heart. He called me to come witness his love for me. He proceeded to get a bowl from the kitchen and placed the sponge in the bowl. He then added water to it. The sponge began to rise and expand. He said, "This is how my love for you grows." I was so touched by that gesture. That memory always stuck with me.

My dad would always have company over, and they would play cards and talk noise to one another. It was a fun-loving atmosphere being around my dad. Unfortunately, he always had extramarital affairs, so my parents' relationship was rocky. He took me everywhere, even to his mistresses' houses. But I didn't understand what was going on because I was always in the rooms, playing with their kids. He and I would drive from New York to North Carolina all the time to visit Mammy and Empi Jones, who were my great-grandparents. I would sleep the whole trip and wake up like clockwork when we arrived.

When my parents divorced, I began to develop the typical "daddy abandonment issues." As a teen, I started looking to older men to fill that father void. Of course, I didn't understand that was what it was that made me seek older guys to have relationships with. According to "T. Rodriguez, *5 Things Every Woman Who Grew Up Without a Father Needs to Know,*" "Researchers have found that fatherless kids have a higher risk of negative outcomes, including poverty, behavioral problems, and lower educational success. The emotional impact of an absentee dad can be long lasting and has the potential to interfere with healthy relationships in adulthood." But my dad was my hero, as far as I was concerned, and I didn't want to hear anything negative about him. Growing up, I always said that if I ever joined the military, I would retire from it just like he did.

MOM

In the early years of my life, I felt my mom was happy. When I had company, she would bring us snacks to eat. I cherished those acts of love and kindness because they made me feel like a special child in my friends' eyes. They would envy me and say, "I wish my mom did that." I would just smile and say, "That's my mom."

The words "I love you" weren't spoken too often in my household after my dad left. Hugs were all but non-existent between my mother and me. Most of the things I remember about my life are clearer in retrospect. I know now that my mother did the best she could with what she had been taught. After all, she didn't have any support from her own mother or father growing up. She was sent to go live with her grandmother in New York. Not speaking much English, she went to school, taught herself English, and became an American citizen. In her adult years she was pretty much a loner and made ends meet the best way she could until she met my dad. By the time I was in my early teens, she had earned a couple of degrees and held a career in the educational field.

She was a teacher, so she was always involved with my teachers and my education. I didn't like that because, no matter who the teacher was, they knew I was Mrs. Jones' child. So needless to say, I couldn't do anything wrong without my mother finding out. There were too many eyes watching me.

I was not an easy child to raise. I started struggling with depression at the early age of 12 when my parents divorced. My mom was always the disciplinarian in my household, and it got worse after the divorce. Her patience and tolerance for my bull was very limited. Giving me a spanking was an understatement. I was no easy spanking candidate, so it made it hard for her to spank me. But even with her small stature, she handled this task all too well. I recall grabbing the belt on many occasions when it would begin to come down on me. She would tell me to turn over, but I just couldn't keep that pose knowing what was about to happen. There were other times she would grab whatever she could find to whoop me. I hated the aftermaths of my whooping. She would say, "If you would be still, you wouldn't get welts and bruising on your arms and legs." She would explain that it hurt her more than it hurt me. I would think, *Really, Mom, how is that even possible?* I was the one who had the welts and bruises and who had endured the whooping. *So how did this hurt you again?*

I was so frightened when she would get mad, especially if we were in the car. At one point in my childhood, I had a mouth full of braces, and if I made her mad, she would smack me so fast I wouldn't see it coming. With my smart mouth and her temper, I would ride in the car with my hand a short distance from my face so I wouldn't get smacked so hard if she got mad at me. I was trying to save the inner lining of my lips from getting cut up by my braces. I did not understand her strict and stern ways. It was like Dr. Jekyll and Mr. Hyde in our household. The only time I really saw a different side of her in my later years was when my friends came over. Everyone loved my mom. They thought she was the sweetest mom to have. I would say to myself, "Boy, does she have them fooled." The boys thought she was a sexy mom. My friends still ask about her today. What an impression she made on them. She was nice to everyone except to me.

MY PARENTS' BREAKUP

As far as I was concerned, I was a happy kid, growing up in a two-parent home, most of my life until the drastic "D-day." My world was shattered, and the mortar that held my foundation together fell apart when my parents decided to get a divorce. I found myself living in a broken home. They gave me no explanation. My dad was just gone. I didn't understand why my parents couldn't stay together and why my dad didn't have communication with me during the breakup. At that time, there were no cellphones, so he couldn't talk to me without going through my mother. At least, that's why he says he didn't contact me. My mother was so hurt that she took to drinking more and more. I recall from time to time sneaking into her medicine cabinet to retrieve her prescription of Diazepam. I took them to help speed up my life, but it didn't work for me, so I quit stealing them. If she knew her pills were missing, she never let me know. I even remember trying to drink a few of her beers, but I didn't like the taste, so I stopped drinking them.

My parents' co-parenting skills were non-existent. My father refused to deal with my mother, which meant he didn't have any communication with me either. As a kid, I interpreted the void as abandonment and was unable to accept myself on a deeper level. I felt worthless and angry. I was convinced that I was not important enough for my dad to explain why he was leaving or to tell me that it didn't reflect on me, that it wasn't my fault. Depression was set into motion in my life. My mom would talk badly about my dad to me, bringing up his extramarital affairs, which didn't help our relationship because resentment started setting in me towards her. I didn't believe what she was saying about my dad. It wasn't until I asked him one day and he admitted it to me that I finally believed it.

This was not an unusual reaction, as it turns out: According to the authors of *The Fatherless Daughter Project*, "In our research we found that at least one in three women see themselves as fatherless. The majority of them felt that losing the bond with their fathers deeply affected multiple areas of their lives, including their emotional and physical health. Their number one fear was being abandoned again, and their main coping mechanism was isolation."

At the age of 15, I became more irritable, judgmental, discontent, depressed, and confused. I wanted to try drugs as a means of escape. I sought out people who could give me something to ease my pain, but I was unsuccessful. This was mainly because in high school I had a 16-year-old boyfriend named King. The name fit because he had that superior presence about him. We met one day when I was at AAA Arcade. This was a game room where the local kids used to hang out. I remember his tall, dark, and handsome physique. I was attracted to his sexiness. His juicy lips were to die for. He had a unique walk that you could spot anywhere. He was also a gun-toting drug dealer who wouldn't give me any drugs. I guess he wanted to protect my innocence, because he would even threaten others that if they gave me any drugs, there would be hell to pay. No one wanted to deal with his wrath. So, I gave up the quest for drugs. When he was shipped off to Job Corps, I began to look toward sex to ease my pain. I had guys coming in and out of my window. There were many times I snuck out my window, walking the streets late at night to go to the arcade.

I dealt with self-isolation and pretty much stayed to myself growing up. The trust was just not there for people in general, as I did not trust or believe in anyone. I was a harsh critic of myself, wallowing in self-loathing and self-rejection. I guess fear that others might leave caused me to guard my heart. I can count the number of close friends I had in high school on one hand. I just wasn't letting people in. I felt trapped and hopeless about my situation. Suicidal thoughts, anger, and depression continued manifesting in my life, and I was ready and eager to leave my mother's house.

Because I was so unhappy in my teens, I jumped on the first chance to leave my mom's household by accepting the first proposal to get married without thinking twice. We had met at the skating rink in Killeen, Texas. Dimitri and another guy would skate around with this little black book, trying to get the numbers of females at the rink. He could really dance on those skates. His medium build and that gap between his two front teeth stole my heart. I didn't care that I was only 17 and he was 21. I thought I was special when he took an interest in me. I was on top of the world. I thought this military man had chosen me, out of all the women he could have, to be his wife. He had put his little black book away for me. So, I married Dimitri, a soldier in the Army. I was so proud that I had married a military man, just like my father. I thought I was set in life.

As an Adult

The marriage did not change the fact that I was unable to accept myself and that I tried to gain acceptance from others. According to I. Cohen, the author of, "How to Let Go of the Need for Approval," from an article in *Psychology Today*, "There will come a time when the constant seeking of approval—the very solution to our problems—will run its course. And that very behavior that brought us so many feelings of accomplishment will become the problem itself." My love and friendships were always conditional, thus causing the second level of my foundation to be unsteady. I did not find what I was looking for in my marriage. My husband was abusive, and I never fought back. I didn't know I could. I was so naive. We were married for a total of four years but separated after only two.

Looking back, I was too young to get married at age 17. My mom had signed for me to get married, despite her better judgment. As for my relationship with my parents, it continued to be distorted. Resentment of my mother continued to grow, and abandonment issues continued to deepen with the absence of my father in my life. Trust in marriage was not developed in my childhood foundation; therefore, trust was always questioned in any relationship I happened to be in.

My depression continued, and I was devastated after I suspected my husband was having an affair. He was my everything. I really had married a man who cheated on me, just as my father had cheated on my mother. I felt so worthless that I had followed in my mother's bad choice of men. But to make matters worse, he was abusive towards me. I had no sisters or brothers to talk to, and I was too embarrassed to talk to my mother until I found myself in a shelter after a bad physical altercation over rumors of an affair with a female soldier. I was happy to just have a roof over my head. But, the living arrangements in the shelter were not comfortable. Looking at the building from the outside, you wouldn't know it was a shelter for battered women. I couldn't stand being there. There were mothers with children, who naturally made a lot of noise. It took me a long time to fall asleep at night. I went back home after staying one day in the shelter. A few days later, Dimitri was gone for several hours, and he wouldn't answer my calls. I felt restless, agitated, and indecisive. I couldn't concentrate. I decided to take my life. I went into my medicine cabinet. I searched drawers and got all the pills I could find in my house, and I took them and lay down to die.

When my husband finally decided to come home from spending time with the same woman he had been seeing at their Charge of Quarters (CQ) post on Fort Hood, he found me in a deeply drugged state. He tried to wake me, but I was too drugged up. My speech was slurred, and I was unable to walk without assistance. He tried giving me juice to drink, but I threw it up. He tried walking me around outside, but my legs seemed to be moving in slow motion. He knew I was in trouble and took me to the hospital. I could hear him telling me not to tell anyone I'd attempted suicide because it would get him in trouble, with him being a soldier and all. I loved him dearly and wanted no trouble for him. So, I lied and told the doctor that I had a really bad headache and was trying to get rid of it with whatever I had in the house. They just looked at me and accepted that answer. I know they knew I was lying but could do nothing about it but treat me. Needless to say, I had to get my stomach pumped. The tube they stuck down my throat made me gag something awful. I lay there with tears running down my face as I watched the mixture of blood and undissolved pills leave my stomach through the tube. My throat was sore for days after that ordeal. That was the most awful experience ever, and I wouldn't wish it on my worst enemy.

It wasn't until five weeks later that I took a pregnancy test, and it was positive. My husband, Dimitri, was so excited at the result that he was going to be a father. I, on the other hand, wasn't too happy. But he convinced me to have the baby. On December 14, 1987, I gave birth to a hairy, beautiful baby girl. At birth she had straight, shiny black hair all over her head. She was fair in complexion and didn't look like either one of us in terms of her shade of color. If I hadn't received her immediately after birth, I would have sworn they gave me the wrong child.

Our daughter wasn't 4 weeks old before my husband got orders to Korea. I was lost and not even sure if I wanted to stay married at this point. This assignment would give us the needed space to figure it out.

I was teetering on the thought of having to raise our daughter alone for a year. I decided to call my mother and ask her if I could move in with her. She said I could come to live with her in Albuquerque, New Mexico, while my husband was deployed to Korea. So, he packed up our stuff and drove to my mother's apartment.

It took about a month for our daughter's hair to begin to curl up, and her shade was caramel in color now. You could see in her facial features the Spanish side of my mother's family. I was full of life again with this bundle of joy the Lord had blessed me with. Motherhood was brand new to me, but with the help of my mother, it went a little smoother.

When my husband had been gone for two months, I went to the hospital for my baby's two-month checkup. I was told that she couldn't be seen and that she was not in the hospital's system. This was odd, because just the previous month she had been seen for her one-month checkup. I was bewildered and went to a group called Waiting Spouses and asked for their help to figure out why my baby couldn't be seen at the military hospital. This is when I found out that my husband was A.W.O.L (Absent Without Leave). He had never shown up for his assignment in Korea. I hated it. I was on my own again, this time with a baby relying on me. I was sickened to know that I would be raising a baby alone without a father. When my husband called to check on us, he acted as if everything were OK. I let him know that I knew he was not in Korea. He told me that my being with my mother was the best thing for the both of us.

When my daughter turned 2 years old, I received notification from my husband's mother that his dad, my daughter's grandfather, had died. I was asked to attend the funeral. I hastily made a round-trip flight to Mississippi to attend the funeral. At the funeral his sister told me that my husband had, in fact, gone to Colorado and impregnated another woman instead of going to Korea. This was another bomb dropped into my lap, and the feeling of abandonment clouded my mind.

After the funeral my husband met with me at his mother's house where I was staying and said, "I didn't want you to find out this way."

"What way?" I asked. "It takes nine months to have a baby, and that child is six months old." My child was two, so he'd had fifteen months to tell me. I hadn't moved; he knew exactly where I was living.

He said, "I felt you were better off with your mother."

I thought that was such a joke. I decided to get a divorce, but I had no clue how to contact him after that. All I knew was that he was living in Colorado with this other woman and their child. So, I contacted a lawyer and told him my dilemma. The lawyer advised me that we could put an ad in the newspaper and petition for a divorce. After a period of time, if there was no response, I could get a divorce through abandonment since I had no clue where he was living. What a relief! That was music to my ears because I wanted to be done with this man. After all, he just up and left his family high and dry. By this time, I had moved into my own apartment across the street from my mother's apartment. I was ready to move on to the next chapter of my life.

CHAPTER TWO

CONTINUING MY ADDICTIVE BEHAVIOR

Did you know?

The eight common behavioral addictions are gambling, sex, internet, shopping, video games, plastic surgery, binge eating disorder/food addiction, and risky behavior? (Liades, 2016).

The disease of addiction manifests itself in many areas of our lives. After I divorced my husband, my addictive behaviors continued. Unhealthy sexual behavior, alcohol, and partying entered my life on a regular basis. I was withdrawn from relationships, overwhelmed by responsibility, and feeling purposeless. Resorting to partying was a means to heal my pain. I found a good babysitter who also lived in our apartment complex. That allowed me to go out clubbing on a regular basis, while working during the day at a Grandy's restaurant as a cashier. I shuffled my new baby to babysitter after babysitter to allow my social life.

I was 21 and going out to nightclubs and partying when I met my second husband, Maxwell. He was high yellow in complexion and had these gorgeous thick lips. I loved slow-dancing with his six-foot slender body. We were a "booty-call relationship" for months before becoming good friends. One day, he came to me and said he was getting kicked out of the Air Force. I told him that if he ever needed a place to stay, he could come to me. Not too long after, he knocked on my door. I opened it up and let him in. I could see the despair written across his face. I asked what was wrong, and he said he needed to take me up on my offer. I said it was no problem, and he asked if he could move in that same day. I was thinking, *Wow*, but I said, "Sure." I wouldn't have offered if I didn't mean it. He lived with me for several months in my one-bedroom apartment. I had a pull-out bed in the living room. So, I gave him the bedroom, and my baby and I slept on the pull-out bed.

It wasn't too long after this incident that I decided to join the military. I was due to turn 22 in three months. Maxwell and I sat down and talked it over and came to an agreement to get married for the benefits. I told him he could continue to live in my Section 8 apartment as long as he took over the full payment and we both got my military benefits while I was shipped off to the Army. I decided to leave my baby with my mother. So, we agreed on a contract marriage. It was an open marriage, meaning that we were married on paper but single in our day-to-day living. He dated or saw who he wanted, and I did the same. I was spiraling out of control, uninterested in sex but using it to my advantage. I was on a quest to manipulate men before they manipulated me. After all, I trusted no one. So, I began down the destructive path of blowing through men like they were toys to be played with, using sex as something casual. Sexual behaviors were at an all-time high in my life.

I suffered from self-destructive thoughts, depression, and constant worrying. I missed my child so dearly.

My assignment in Belgium was for three years. Halfway into my assignment, the military gave me permission to have my family with me. So, I flew back to the States and got my daughter and Maxwell and brought them to Belgium to live with me. Maxwell got a job working at the local post exchange (PX) as a cashier/stocker. On one payday he decided to do the unthinkable. He stashed a couple of pairs of jeans behind the store near the dumpster. His plan was to retrieve them later when he got off work and take them home. But he was seen on the surveillance camera performing the theft. He was arrested and was held until I could get him out of jail. My commanding officer made it clear to me that I was responsible for this man's actions and that I could be punished for this. I was embarrassed, humiliated, and furious that he would jeopardize my career when he had the money to pay for the jeans.

I was through with him and wanted a divorce. He didn't fight me, and we got a non-contested divorce. Our relationship was ended after two and a half years of marriage.

After this, I never took anyone seriously, guarding my heart and staying withdrawn, or so I thought until a long-time friend named Diablo took a more serious interest in me and proposed. He was one of the men I'd had an off-and-on fling with. He saw the ups and downs, the twist and turns I went through. He witnessed my tricking behavior and still accepted me. I didn't accept the proposal the first time. I was not really physically attracted to him, but he was a fun person to be around. I saw him as only a friend.

Diablo was determined to sway me to marry him, so he invited me on a trip to Spain. I accepted. It was so enjoyable, and I got to be my funny, witty self without masking who I was. We grew closer as friends. He treated my daughter just like she was his own kid. He looked after her all the time while I had to work. He taught her how to ride a bike and skate. He spent quality time with her. I cherished that, because that type of connection is what I always wanted with my own father. That was the act that won me over. He adored me and my child, and that was enough to say yes to his proposal. But I held off letting him in. I continued to mask my feelings of self-loathing and decreased self-esteem, even as they grew. Even though I was not in love with him, I liked him for my daughter. I thought that with him loving me and my daughter, I could eventually fall in love with him, too. A few months later, he proposed again, and I said, "Yes." I got married for the third time at the age of 26. Even though this was a joyous occasion, I couldn't help beating myself up for being married three times before the age of 30. I told myself this had to be the last marriage because if it didn't last, my track record would become 0-3. And I wasn't getting any younger.

Starting my Military Career

During my military career, the second layer of my foundation began to crumble. I faced many obstacles being a woman in the Army, and being a black one at that. I felt I always had to prove myself worthy of promotions. I had to get the higher ranking to take me seriously and to give me the opportunity to show my talents and skills. It was a challenge to show them that I had what it took to be in charge. I welcomed that challenge and proved myself worthy of the position every time. I studied and improved my technical skills also, thus proving that I had what it took to do my job unsupervised. I played hard and worked hard. I was on a mission to be successful in the Army.

My job title was Microwave System Maintainer (31P). I competed against men all the time. I was very athletic and competitive. I always made sure I did my best in all areas of my military career, not giving anyone reason to find blame in me. I stayed in civilian schools to improve my General Technical (GT) score and obtained my associate's degree, then my bachelor's degree, and finally my master's degree. I was committed to staying in the military and retiring just like my dad had. I took on several positions that were above my grade level on a regular basis. I moved up the ranks pretty quickly.

I kept my personal life separate from my military life. After all, I was out of control, dating people who could benefit me. I can recall having one guy buying groceries while another bought me flowers all the time. Life was exciting again for me. I dated mostly civilians and not military personnel. Looking back, throughout my twenty years of active duty, I never found anyone who was dedicated in the relationship, to include my current husband, except for God. I traveled many places, such as the East Coast (Virginia, Maryland, and Washington, D.C.), Georgia, Belgium, Korea, and Turkey throughout my time in the Army.

By now I had lost communication with my dad. I was still looking for acceptance from him. I retrieved his phone number from his sister and decided to reach out to him again. We finally had a lasting communication about staying in touch. He recognized his mistakes and wished to seek forgiveness and restore the relationship. I was so overjoyed to have my father back in my life again, even though I was already an adult. It was like I was that 12-year-old all over again.

I had made it to the rank of specialist (SPC), E-4, when I got married for the third time. We flew to the States and got married by a justice of the peace in Virginia, with my dad as a witness. We later had a church wedding in Belgium, where we were living. We had two singers and a biblical poem on "Love" read. My dress was white, a mermaid style forming to the shape of my body.

Financial Issues and Spending

I expected my new husband to give me the love and acceptance I couldn't give to myself. Although he wanted me to get out of the military, I stuck it out. I made it to the rank of sergeant (SGT), E-5. It felt like he was in competition with me since we both were in the military and he was still a specialist, E-4. This put a strain on the marriage constantly. However, my reason for romantic involvement was based on a desire to share my life with an equal partner and mainly to have a father for my child. I thought I'd found that in him.

We got stationed to the Pentagon in Washington, D.C., and life in this marriage was rough. My dad lived two hours away in Richmond, Virginia, so not only could we talk, but we could now visit one another. My faith in God was growing, and I started to attend church on a regular basis.

During this time my husband kept pressuring me to have another child. I was dead set against this idea. Plus, it was rumored that he was having affairs before I got there to D.C., so that lingered in my head all the time. The bricks started tumbling down in my foundation again. I was confused about the direction I wanted to go in with this marriage. I had a fractured heart once again, and I never wanted to have another kid, especially not with this man. I'd made this clear from day one. But that was his dream, and I couldn't fulfill that for him.

The marriage was explosive and volatile most days, even when we went to church. Because of adultery on both our parts, the marriage ended in deeper resentment. He impregnated another woman, who was also an usher in our church. That was a spiritual crush for me and the last straw for both of us. Going through the divorce, we fought over everything except my daughter. He just backed up off of her like he had never been a part of her life. What a tragedy for both me and my daughter. I never would have imagined him turning his back on her the way he did. This is something I will regret all my life because I'd brought him into her life. I am plagued with guilt over not being as responsible or committed as I should have been. But you can't change what has already happened. And you can't make anyone do anything.

I thought, "Where is my God?" Loneliness set in, with many days of suicidal thoughts. I can recall one day when I wrote in my journal about my suicidal thoughts. On December 4, 2001, I wrote, "Once again I find myself thinking about ending my life. But you know God gave me my child for that reason, I believe. I am so disappointed with my life. I hate everything right now. I'm trying to hold it together, but it is getting harder by the day. Sometimes I just want to say to heck with it and let everything just go [referring to my house]. I tried so hard to do what is right, but it seems that my worst fear will come true and that is losing this house. Well, I've tried. I also want to be in love, and I want someone to love me so much that he will never cheat, flirt, or disrespect me in any way. I guess that is asking too much in this lifetime."

This marriage lasted seven and a half years. I was stuck with all the bills and the responsibility of selling the house. My debt crisis had weakened me. I regretted accumulating so much debt in the marriage. According to EJ Rawes, author of the study "Top 5 Money Problems Americans Face" from *USA Today*, "The average household's credit card debt exceeds $7,000." In addition to this debt, Americans may find themselves worrying about mortgages, car loans, car insurance, and student loans. Last year, according to Money-Rates from the *Wall Street Journal*, their survey, "found that 8 percent of people feel that paying student loans is their biggest financial worry."

I wondered if my debt would render me powerless. It was a plus that Diablo had to pay me alimony for two years, as well as child support, because he had adopted my child.

Once again, my sexual escapades continued.

While in the military, I often took on additional jobs as a security officer supervisor or as an office mover, moving office furniture and boxes for additional cash. I took these jobs not because I needed the money but because I was a workaholic. I found pleasure in working and spending excessive money. This kept me busy and preoccupied mentally. I was a workaholic for a number of years after my failed third marriage, sometimes working up to three jobs at a time. On days I didn't work an extra job, I would go to my military job early and stay late after everyone had gone home. It was an emotional outlet for me. According to J. Graves's article, *"17 Signs You Might Be a Workaholic,"* "Being committed to and passionate about your job are good qualities, but there's a distinction between having a strong work ethic and being a workaholic." I didn't watch my kid grow up or anything. She practically raised herself, and I am not proud of that, but I would be damned if another man was going to leave me financially stuck in a pit.

I made a lot of things more important than living. Did I have to work? Yes. But I should have done it in moderation, especially since I was a single mom raising a kid. And there is where I planted the seed of resentment between my daughter and me. She became resentful of not having a dad physically and not having a mom mentally or physically. I made work my life.

It was July of 2002. While still in the military I was stationed at Fort Gordon, Georgia. By now my daughter was 14 years old, and she was starting high school. My job in the military as a technical writer afforded me the capability of working a day schedule. I was at it again, frequenting nightclubs on the weekends. All I was doing was making my heart harder and harder and growing deeper in alcoholism. I never thought I had a problem because I didn't drink beer like my mother, and I wasn't even drinking hard liquor, only wine. I remember one day when my daughter came in my room and said to me, "You're drinking that nasty red stuff again." I just yelled at her to get out of my room because I was angry that she called me out. I was clearly addicted to alcohol. I was sick and tired of pain. I was tired of these failed relationships and feared men and relationships at this point. I second-guessed my own opinion, while still remaining self-obsessed over my wants and needs through people, places, and things. My reactions were resentment, anger, and fear, which make up the triangle of self-obsession: resentment of my past, anger about my present, and fear of my future. Unable to accept myself, I tried to gain acceptance through others. I was in denial that my life had become unmanageable. I was living in depression and self-rejection. I did anything I had to in order to gain that acceptance and approval, and then I resented those who wouldn't respond the way I wanted them to.

My photos with Presidents Obama and Bush

Four years had passed when I got promoted to staff sergeant (SSG), E-6. My military career continued to blossom. I had fifteen years in the military under my belt when I was selected to the White House in Washington, D.C. I was a dedicated, hardworking soldier who lived a secret life during my off time.

Three years later my daughter gave me the news that I was going to be a grandma. I was distraught because I always wanted more for my daughter than to be a single parent like me and my mother before me. But after the birth of my granddaughter, I was on cloud nine. My granddaughter looked like a little baby doll with her thick, curly black hair. She was a healthy baby. She rarely cried. She smiled all the time, even in her sleep. It was so exciting to watch. For the next several years I was a happy nana. My daughter worked as a pharmacy technician at CVS pharmacy. I was so proud of her for her career path.

This was also about the time I was promoted to sergeant first class (SFC), E-7. I was assigned to the White

House Communication Agency in Washington, D.C. I traveled with the president, vice president, and first lady to locations such as Texas, Louisiana, Georgia, Alabama, Honduras, and Kazakhstan, to name just a few. My time at the White House was the most exciting time of my military tour of duty (the second being my tour of Turkey). I was promoted to the role of noncommissioned officer in charge (NCOIC) of the White House Situation Room (WHSR). There were many celebrities who came to visit, and we got to see them and show them around the WHSR and explain what our unique job description was.

Here, I am standing next to Brad
Pitt in the Situation Room.

Excess Eating

During my fourth year in the White House, I was asked to extend my tour of duty there for an additional two years. I accepted since I held the position of NCOIC of the WHSR. I was in charge of eight people: two civilians, three Air Force soldiers, two Navy soldiers, and one Army soldier. But it was really political, and I faced racism, especially from my supervisor in the Situation Room. He was an officer in the Air Force. He had blue eyes that looked like a shark's dead stare. Every chance he got, he was looking for a way to replace me with a particular white female soldier. Finally, the opportunity came. I had continued to travel on many occasions, and during my fifth year, I injured my back lifting up equipment-filled boxes. I was put on opiates for the pain in my lower back. The injury I sustained was a herniated disk in the SI-L5 area. It wasn't too long after that I was told I was a "risk" by my shark-eyed supervisor because of the pain meds. He said I would have to resign my position as the NCOIC of the WHSR. I was furious and refused to resign. Instead, I chose to retire since I had twenty years and fourteen days of military time under my belt.

Betrayal and depression flooded my life once again. I began taking the pills in excess—one to manage the physical pain I felt and two to numb the mental thought of being a failure. My foundation had crumbled from beneath me. Now, not only was I out of the military, but I was addicted to pain pills and got them by any means necessary. No mortar or bricks could put back these pieces. I frequently visited the psychiatrist for my depressed mental state and visited my primary doctor because now I was confined to a walker. I could not work extra jobs, and I began eating excessively. I gained weight in the extreme. My back was hurting more and more. I faced what were referred to as psychological risk factors. According to D. Preiato, author of *7 Harmful Effects of Overeating*, "Depression and binge eating are strongly linked. Many binge eaters are either depressed or have been before; others may have trouble with impulse control and managing and expressing their feelings. Low self-esteem, loneliness, and body dissatisfaction may also contribute to binge eating."

My opiate addiction continued to grow, so much so that I would even buy pills off the street. Other drugs hadn't yet crossed my mind, but I had to have my pain pills, sometimes in excess. I even had an older gentleman getting pills from other veterans for me. He was an enabler in my life. He would also bring food and encourage me to eat my sorrows away. And that I did. Every chance I got, I ordered carryout or went to a buffet. The heated seats in my SUV made it easy for me to drive without pain. Buffets were my pastime. While retired, the military disability considered me housebound. Housebound meant that, due to my injury, I could not get a nine-to-five job outside of my house. I was unable to work because sitting and standing for periods of time caused excruciating pain. I got paid extra disability because of it. But that had me feeling worthless because all I ever wanted was to retire from the military, work another job, and retire from that job, too. In my current condition, that dream would not happen. I felt like a failure. I was a hard worker, and working was all I knew. Not needing to work another day of my life, I was still in great despair. Not being able to work was a slap in my face. I hated my life, and I felt no use in it. I felt I was a waste of air. *What purpose do I have now?* I asked myself. *What do I do with myself?* I decided I needed a change of atmosphere because everything in D.C. reminded me of what I could never be. Plus, I couldn't even do most jobs with my back injury. Sitting or standing was a problem for me.

CHAPTER THREE

....

FEELINGS THAT LED TO USING

Did you know?

Seven common reasons people use drugs are genetic vulnerability, cultural attitudes, financial incentives, personality, self-medication, and loneliness (Heshmat, 2017).

LIFE AS A VETERAN

Health issues

My health was deteriorating, and my weight was increasing. Another brick was falling out of my rocky foundation. The Veterans Administration (VA) considered my back injury to be an unfixable chronic issue. Suffering from this chronic back pain affected every area of my life. I had fallen into one of the excuses that cause people to use drugs in the first place. I had lost my confidence in God to help me. I was suffering from a spiritual void. I felt like I was in a spiritual vacuum, empty inside. Through other failed relationships, I felt God had given up on me because I had given up on myself. I had a great deal of self-doubt. I felt tired, hopeless, and lifeless most of the time. Then the VA hospital said that opiates were an epidemic that needed to be controlled. Cold turkey, they stopped the issuing of all opiates to patients with pain issues, even chronic pain patients such as myself. In hindsight, that was the best thing that could have happened to me. I began the slow withdrawal from my addiction to opiates for pain. My back was still hurting regularly. I was using my walker daily.

Because D.C. was such a fast-paced city, in 2013 I decided to move to Texas and left my 26-year-old daughter behind. My mother was living in Texas, in the same town my parents got a divorce in. So off to Killeen, Texas, I went. I moved in with my mother. My mother had mellowed out some. Her relationship with my daughter was no comparison to our relationship. She was more patient with my daughter and granddaughter. But still we couldn't get along, so I moved out within two months.

The transition to Texas seemed to do me some good. The slow-paced lifestyle was a blessing in disguise. The warm temperatures were a change to the D.C. weather. I could walk around the neighborhood with my walker on a continuous sidewalk. I didn't miss the D.C. cracks in the sidewalk. I purchased a single-level, four-bedroom house and was living the suburban life. My body was feeling much better, but in 2015, my weight was at an all-time high. I was disgusted with the way my face and body looked. I hated life. I hated the shortness of breath I had from just walking in my own house. I couldn't work due to my back, and I was miserably fat. I couldn't find joy in anything. I didn't want anyone to see me. I had been skinny all my life, so this was outrageous to me. I couldn't accept myself, so how could I expect anyone else to accept me? I was so disgusted in my appearance. My face was round and full.

Six months passed when my daughter and grand-daughter joined me in Texas and were living with me in the house. I was happy to have them there. My daughter cooked every day, and my granddaughter did housework. They were the added help I needed. But thoughts of my weight consumed my mind.

After a long decision-making process, I decided to have gastric bypass surgery to control my weight. I was excited and couldn't wait to get this weight off. I did not have to lose any weight before surgery like most patients had to because of their size. It was set; the surgery would be done in San Antonio, Texas. My daughter drove me to and from the surgery. I was not scared until the day of the surgery, especially when the chaplain came and asked me if I wanted him to pray for me. My fears weren't relieved until the doctor came to see me before the surgery and signed my stomach where the surgery would take place. I was reassured that no other procedure would be performed on me.

This surgery relieved a lot of my pain issues by taking the excess weight off. I was enjoying life again, hanging with my high school friends at the club and other events on occasion. But one day, the pain started coming back into my lower back. I was issued a new walker. By 2018, my legs just started going numb for no reason, and I couldn't operate my lower extremities. I was then issued a wheelchair and put on non-opiate pain meds. They were slow-acting and really didn't help with the numbness in my legs. I couldn't walk or get around without help. That's when I ran into a long-time high school classmate named PJ.

Depression can cripple an otherwise remarkable person, and I was living with feelings of abandonment, three failed marriages, broken friends and family ties, and not being able to fulfill my second job retirement goal. Even positive emotions caused stressors in my life. There could not be anyone more precious to me than my mother. But even though we were in the same state, we didn't talk much, and that stressed me out. There was no shortage of other stressful events, to include my mother's and my unresolved anger in our relationship, which contributed to my emotional breakdown. I had unrealistic expectations of another person and a lack of open communication in my immediate family relationships. I was stressed about not having a job and feeling my life was unpredictable or my future was uncertain. This was perfectionism at its worst.

This can't be how life is supposed to be, I thought. I just had a negative outlook on everything. I started looking for a way out. By now I felt suicide was not an option, especially since I had my granddaughter living with me. But when my daughter and granddaughter moved into their own apartment, I was happy for them. My daughter was standing on her own two feet. But I was alone again. I needed to escape my life, and I needed to escape both my mental and physical pain.

I decided to try to occupy my time by attending school. I went to school at Central Texas College (CTC) for medical billing and coding. Since my disability did not permit me to hold a job outside my house, my plan was to finish schooling and work from home in the medical billing and coding field.

Introduction to drugs

One day, after school, I was sitting on my rocking chair on my front porch when a longtime high school friend drove by on the way to his mother's house. His mother lived a couple of streets from my house. I couldn't believe it was PJ. He looked the same, except he was much skinnier. You could see his cheekbones protruding from his face. His ethnicity was half Black and half Korean. He had the prettiest long, black wavy hair.

PJ was known for his reputation of being an addict. Through him, I found an opportunity to escape, a new way of dealing with my sorrows and pain. Little did I know that having PJ in my life would be my downfall, a long spiral to my rock bottom. My reliance on God had decreased tremendously, and the brickwork in my life ceased to exist during this period of time. Now, PJ was homeless and needed a place to stay. I offered to let him rent out one of my rooms. On a daily basis, he saw how I struggled just to get around in my own house. He asked, "Why won't the VA hospital help you with medication that will help you with your pain?" I said they thought what they had given me would be sufficient to aid my ailments without causing any addiction. It wasn't long before we began on a drug quest to find a solution to help with my pain. It turned out that his motive was to get me to use my money to support his drug habit and not really to help me. At this point, we were using each other for drugs.

Before PJ, I had already had experience with alcohol, pain pills (Percocet, OxyContin, Vicodin), and weed (in food—gummies and crispy rice bars).

With PJ I got into cocaine: smoking primos (tobacco laced with heroin) and sniffing. I also did heroin (known as 8 balls or bars on the street), smoked crystal meth (known as ice on the street), and smoked PCP (known as dip or wet on the street). I finally found something I liked, and it was on and popping. Wet was my drug of choice. I liked the way it made me feel. I had no care in the world. I felt stronger after I would black out. When I would come to, I had so much energy and strength. I felt no pain when I used. I felt no mental anguish when I used. I was hooked. I constantly experienced racing thoughts of how I could get rid of PJ and break away and score.

I wanted to score on my own, but I had no "plug" (drug dealer connection). I was looking to get one because I was tired of going through PJ to get my drugs. He always wanted some of what I got, as if my money were his money. I can recall one night going to get wet, which is embalming fluid mixed with PCP, with PJ, Fred, and Reuben. Fred was another addict that hung with PJ. He became my friend, too, at least for that night. We had to pick up Reuben, the person who actually had the connection that we needed to cop the drugs. He said he had a plug who lived in Cameron, Texas. It took a while before the plug had the time to meet with us. We were desperate, so we sat in the car and waited. By the time he could meet it was dark, but I wanted what I wanted.

So, Fred, Reuben, PJ, and I headed to Cameron for our drug quest. I had $100 with me, just enough to buy what I wanted. When we got to Cameron, PJ jumped out of the car as if he had money. Keep in mind, this was my first time going with them to get drugs, so all this was unfamiliar. The plug sent his girlfriend to meet us at a store parking lot to check us out. PJ went up to her car, then she came and got in our car. She wanted us to smoke one, I guess to test us. So, PJ turned to me and told me to give her five dollars. I reluctantly gave it to her because I only had the $100 to purchase my wet. I looked at them and asked them where their money was. Between the two of them, they had no money and expected to swindle me out of my money to get high. PJ told Fred that I was going to share what I got with them. Well, that was not my intention. Who does that? Addicts who try to get over on others do. Now I was short five dollars and I was pissed.

The plug called his girlfriend and told her where we were to meet him to buy the drugs. We drove to a dark park in Temple, Texas, and waited. When the plug pulled up, PJ told me to give him $100 and he would go do the exchange because the plug did not know me and might get suspicious. I didn't trust him, so I got out, too. He fussed at me and told me I was going to scare the plug off. I didn't believe what he was saying, and I got out anyway. Well, sure enough, the plug was hesitant when he saw me, but he wanted to do the deal since he had driven all the way from Cameron to meet us. I told him I didn't have the full $100 because of them smoking my five dollars at the store. At first, he didn't want to do the deal, but after talking to him for a while and exchanging numbers with him so I could purchase straight from him in the future, he agreed. He sold me a bottle of embalming fluid laced with PCP.

Before we could even get out of Temple, PJ was asking me to dip into my bottle. Reluctantly I allowed them to. We started back towards home, but we had to drop Reuben back home. He was so high he forgot where he lived, so we ended up driving around for an hour before he agreed to let us drop him off across the street from the VA hospital. When he got out, PJ and Fred proceeded to drive me back home, but not before asking for another dip into my bottle. I refused. PJ said I was being selfish because I wouldn't share my drugs. Imagine that. PJ used my money to purchase his high, so I didn't feel the slightest bit bad. After all, they had already hit my stash twice.

That was the last time I went through or supported PJ's drug venture, and I was also able to get him to move out of my house, with great resistance. I had his parents force him to move out. I now drove to Cameron and met the plug on my own. One day, when I was supposed to meet my friends at the club, I had smoked one wet too many, because I was instantly put into a comatose state. My legs and arms became numb, and I couldn't move my entire body. I lay there wishing I could operate my arm and my legs, but I couldn't. I didn't know which way I was going or coming. I feared for my life because I was home alone, with no one to help me. I thought that if this is the way death felt, I didn't want it. I lay there silent and desolate. It seemed like an eternity passed. I prayed that I would move again. But I lay there until I just fell asleep. Little did I know, it was only the beginning.

PART II

During the Grips of My Addiction

Did you know?

There are several examples of federal drug charges under 21 U.S.C. 844 that could fall under the DEA's jurisdiction, including drug trafficking, drug manufacturing, possession of a controlled substance, and drug conspiracy. (Goldstein & Orr, n.d.).

Temporary loss of sanity

The third layer of my brickwork continued to fall off and lay on the floor when I was experiencing wet. One day when I was in the bathroom of my house doing wet, a slow chill went through my body as darkness fell all around me. I was trapped inside a figment of my imagination. It felt as if the innermost part of my face had reversed to the back side of my head, and I physically could not see any more. It took on a dimension of reality that I was lost inside my head. My eyes no longer appeared in their eye sockets. It was like going through a maze, and I had to find the way out. Yet the maze was in my head, and it was dark, so I couldn't see anything in front of me. I had to feel my way out. I couldn't find my way. I knew I was in my bathroom, but I had no vision. It was pure darkness. My eyes and mind were locked in a maze. I didn't like feeling so overpowered and helpless. My mind was an unidentifiable blur inside a black abyss. Alone in that darkness, I searched for the opening of my eye sockets so I could see again. I talked to God, asking him to please give me my sight. I made all sorts of quitting promises. And suddenly, the dark dungeon vanished, and my mind was unlocked. The lights from my bathroom appeared far off in the distance. I followed the light and regained my sight. My mind was restored to normalcy, and it felt like the innermost part of my face reversed back to the front of my head. That was such a scary experience. I thought I had lost my sight forever. But I thank God, who is my trowel, that He saw fit to heal me undeservedly.

Even after this ordeal, I continued to look for people I could get my drug of choice from, since Cameron, Texas, was so far to travel. I asked this guy named JC. I had known him for about a year. JC was in my peer support group at the VA hospital.

I knew JC smoked weed on the regular, so I figured he might know a connection. He said he was going to Houston and could get wet for me, but there was one stipulation. I would have to use it at his house so that I wasn't alone in case anything happened. I felt after knowing him for a year and visiting his house on several occasions that he could be trusted, so I agreed. I just wanted the fix, and plus it was going to be New Year's at midnight and I didn't want to be alone.

He picked me up and we arrived at his house. He rolled a joint and we shared it, but I wanted my wet. He got the wet from his refrigerator. There were two of them wrapped in aluminum foil. He placed them on the table. I immediately opened the wrapping. I lit one and put the other one in my purse while he was pulling the steaks out the refrigerator.

Finally, he had given the wet to me, and I was a happy camper. He tried to ration it to me and went in my purse and took the other one back from me when I wasn't looking. When I realized it was gone, I overlooked it because I knew I was going to smoke it later anyway. He cooked dinner while I watched TV. In between the cooking, we managed to smoke three more joints before I asked for something more comfortable to wear. By now he had invited me to stay over in his extra room. I agreed since I was having so much fun listening to music, watching TV, doing my wet, and smoking joints. He gave me a jersey shirt. We smoked another joint and I lost some time, but I didn't know this until he told me he had to take me outside to get some air to bring me back. I couldn't walk so well. I recall saying something like, "I can't walk." But it was a blur. I just didn't clearly recall. He smoked another joint and I didn't.

By now I was craving wet again, so he finally gave me the second one. I was so excited. I was still mad that he'd taken it out of my purse to control when I could have it. I smoked it and blacked out. When I came to, he was lying behind me and raping me. I asked him what he was doing, and he stopped. He said he thought I had overdosed, and he thought he was going to have to take me to the hospital. I saw the bowl of water and washcloth he said he was using to cool me down. But I guess somehow in his cooling me down he got turned on and then decided to rape me while I was under the influence of my blackout state. How sickening—it's like having sex with a dead person. But I was still so out of it, I was in no position to go home. So, I stayed and pretended nothing had happened.

When he took me home the following morning, the reality of what had happened set in. I had been raped by a so-called friend. We had the same peer support counselor at the VA hospital. I told the counselor what had happened and that I couldn't be his patient any longer because I was fearful that I might see that man again. That was the last time I ever saw the man who had raped me.

CHAPTER FOUR

INSTITUTIONS, HOSPITALIZATIONS, AND JAILS

Did you know?

Each year in the U.S., there are nearly 100,000 emergency hospitalizations for adverse drug events in adults 65 and older, says researcher Daniel S. Budnitz, MD, MPH, director of the CDC's Medication Safety Program (Doheny, 2011).

Emergency Room

A few days after the rape I had confused feelings about the rape on Jan 1. Was it rape, or did I consent during my blackout? If I hadn't used drugs, I wouldn't have been in that situation at all. I was feeling bad about the situation and wanted to harm myself. I felt suicidal and in despair after having been raped. I had a high level of guilt and regret for trusting a person who didn't have my best interests at heart. I constantly engaged in negative self-talk. I took the bus to the Veterans Administration emergency room, where I was placed in a steel room with hard plastic furniture. It had one plastic bed and a plastic chair. I knew where I was headed, and I welcomed it because I yearned for the help. According to a report by P. Owens on *Healthcare Costs Utilization Project,* "Emergency departments (EDs) have been identified as an important site of care to identify individuals at risk, to provide timely support and intervention, and to facilitate entry into more intensive treatment, if appropriate."

There I was in the ER, and I had unmet needs, wants, and desires. I was at an all-time low, and I knew that medical treatment would get me out of my current situation and give me a peaceful environment. At home, I had been arguing with my daughter and mother on the regular. I lay on the bed waiting. I know the ER staff were trained to assess the level of lethality and could manage my care. I waited for the referral to the psych ward to take place. I appeared to be alone in a dimly lit dungeon, being monitored outside my room by the medical staff. I understood the monitoring, but I didn't like it at all. I felt like a caged animal. Not truly alone, I continued to sense the presence of other patients and medical staff. There was another patient next door who also had a police officer monitoring her. She was cussing him out and threatening him. It kind of took the pressure off being in that locked-up room. They were comical, to say the least. My desire to suppress the need to cry was at an all-time high. I continued to listen to the conversation next door between the police officer and that patient. She said, "Pig, you roughed me up. That was unnecessary." He replied that he had done what was necessary. She was calling him names, and he was telling her that she was right where she needed to be. She even referenced his small manhood and how he thought he was a big man handling a woman. They kept going back and forth with each other. By now the drugs in my system were causing my legs to go numb. I couldn't walk. They kept me and started paperwork to transfer me to the psych ward so I could be monitored with a thorough psych evaluation.

Psych ward

After I was admitted to the psych ward, I began to have a seizure, and my legs and arms began to convulse. My arms and legs began to move rapidly on their own. I tried to control them, but it was like they had a mind of their own. The staff tried to hold me down and keep me from convulsing. They snatched the mattress off the bed and placed it on the floor so I wouldn't hurt myself and fall off the bed. I lay there while my whole body jerked and convulsed. The staff came to check on me about every ten minutes, but I was still twitching, jerking, and rocking. It seemed like hours that my hands and legs continued to move rapidly. The doctor on call came in to check on me. He advised the nurse to give me some sort of sedative. It calmed my jerking legs and arms. After that, my body was so sore it felt like I had been working out. Another phase set in. My legs were going numb, and I couldn't move them. I was confined to a wheelchair for the rest of my stay.

Everything in the psych ward was violence proof and suicide proof. The toilets in the room didn't even have a toilet seat. The bed, chair, and desk were that hard plastic that was too heavy to move or throw. My stay was rough because of the illness, but good for me. I don't have any regrets about the choices I made or my willingness to go to the psych ward to begin with. It was the best place for me to be at that time, with the best help possible. Someone had to figure out what was wrong with me, as I clearly couldn't. At the psych ward, they adjusted my antidepressant medication and determined that my leg numbness was due to drug-induced neuropathy, meaning that the drugs in my system were causing the numbness in my legs, thus causing me to be confined to a wheelchair. I stayed there ten long days, using the wheelchair everywhere I went. I even had to have a shower chair placed in my shower when I wanted to bathe.

After the psych evaluation and when my legs had regained their functionality, I was recommended to the Serious Mental Illness Life Enhancement (SMILE) program. This program was for mentally disturbed people to help them reenter the world. It is a psychiatric facility that provides inpatient psychiatric care for veterans with substance abuse problems. The primary focus of this program is to improve the quality of life for veterans, promoting independence and recovery. Even though I was put on antidepressants, it seemed that my suicidal ideation got worse. After the completion of the program, I was released to my home.

DWI and jail

One day after my release from the SMILE program, I decided that I couldn't continue to attend school, especially since I had missed so much class. I took my medication and headed to the campus of Central Texas College. On the way, my medication kicked in, but I kept on driving because I was determined to accomplish my withdrawal. When I reached the campus, I got pulled over because the campus police officer said I was swerving on the campus roads. He was a real jerk about it, and you could tell he was gung-ho on arresting me like he was on some quota for arrests. I told him I hadn't done any drugs, just that my medicine took effect sooner than I had expected. He arrested me anyway and had my car towed.

We waited for the Gatesville police to come to take me to the hospital to see if I was medically cleared to go to jail. Also, they were sure that I had drugs in my system, but the doctor told them I didn't. They were just trying to pile on more charges. I said, "I told you it was my medication that had affected me in that way." So, once I was medically cleared, they took me to Coryell County Jail in Gatesville, booked me, and I received my first DWI charge.

I remained there until they transferred me to Bell County. This jail was well equipped and nicer than any jail I had been to. We had inside recreation for individuals and outside recreation by cell block. The inside recreation area had exercise equipment and a ping-pong table, and the outside recreation had a basketball court and hoop. They gave me the full dosage of my medication that the Veterans Administration had in my medical files. The staff treated you like humans. And the physiologist visited often. That's where I met Man. The name fit because she carried herself like a man. She wore her pants sagging below her waist and had a close-cut haircut like a guy's hairstyle. She often joked that I was her "jail wife." I didn't take to that too kindly. At least I hoped she was joking, because I don't swing that way.

But I just laughed it off. She looked after me and was so friendly. I thought she was a good person, so we exchanged information. I remained in Bell County for two days and was released on a personal recognizance (PR) bond.

My run with addicts

After Man got out of jail, she called me and we met up. I was so glad to see her. After all, she had taken care of me when I was in jail. However, I knew she liked me, or at least she saw me as another lick. According to the Online Slang Dictionary, a lick is a means to make money, especially illegally. I had "naive" stamped on my forehead. I guess that is why she took me to this particular house to get drugs one day.

Upon entering, I noticed several men in various rooms, and one by one they would come out to get something from the kitchen. After sitting on the sofa, this lady came out and I greeted her. She responded and quickly made her way back to one of the back rooms. I stayed sitting on the couch while another younger girl came out with a man and was kissing on him. The girl went back to the room and the woman came out, calling that same man "baby". I was floored. It looked like all the men and these two ladies were all coupled up, or should I say each man was involved in a ménage à trois.

Man was talking to people outside the house. I stepped outside to see what was going on out there. When I stepped to her, she asked me for my money. I was holding it in my hand at this point, but I refused to give it to her. She snatched my money out of my hand and began swearing at me. The owner of the house made it clear to her that her behavior toward me would not be tolerated at his home. She gave me my money back and told me we had a connection across the street she would handle for me. In my stupidity, I gave the guys across the street my money, and they gave Man my drugs. It was not my drug of choice they gave, however. It was more coke. In this switch-up, she stole my money again and got her drugs in the process. She was a true addict, manipulating the situation at every turn.

I was furious. I kept going back and forth with the guy, telling him he stole my money, first because he didn't give me what I asked for, and second because he gave Man the drug of her choice with my money. I went back in the house and then these three dudes came inside and were basically trying to get me high for sexual favors. Hell, no! I was not going to be bought, bartered, or sold for her high. That's when I knew she meant me no good ever. How dare she send them in the house, I thought. When they realized I wasn't cooperative, they left me alone. Thank goodness, because they could have overpowered me and taken what they wanted. I came back outside and sat next to this guy who had witnessed all this mess this woman had taken me through. By then I just wanted to go home. He offered to take me home, and although I did not know him, I jumped at the offer. He drove straight to my house as we talked along the way. He was so down to earth with his conversation. He told me that when he saw me, he knew I didn't belong there. I agreed that I was out of my element.

Some time went by, and when I had an appointment at the VA hospital, I ran into Man again. She apologized and promised this time she would take me to try to find my drug of choice, wet. I was desperate because I hadn't had my drug of choice and really wanted it. She said it was best if she drove since she knew the way around. Like a dummy, I let her drive. We went to several houses until we came across a particular one. I stayed in the car when she went in. When she came out, she and another girl were arguing. The girl said she owed her money. Man said the other man could get what I wanted. I asked how much Man owed. She said five dollars, so I said we would go to the ATM and be back. When we came back from the ATM, I wouldn't give her my money because she had stolen from me before.

I went in the house with her and I paid the lady, and immediately she gave it to another girl for exchange for a rock. Little did I know I was in a crack house. People were sitting around with their stem waiting for someone to share the drug they acquired. They were drifters who latched on to the free drugs that come with someone on a bender. They pulled out the stem and shared a hit. Of course, Man took several drags off of the stem and so did I. But the guy couldn't get what I wanted.

We left and went on to another house for what I wanted, or so I thought. But then the car crash happened. On the way, Man sideswiped a tree and wrecked my car and tore off the mirror also. We got into an argument. I told her to get out. She jumped out and took my remote for my car with her. I was stranded there at a closed store. I slept in my car using boxes I had in the car to cover me up for the night. When morning came, I called my daughter to bring the spare remote. I was finally fed up with this woman. I had to find another way of maintaining my drug habit.

DWI and jail continue

A few days passed, and I was arrested again because the bond company revoked my bond after I received a second DWI while trying to get a bottle of wet at a truck stop in Waco. I was meeting my Cameron plug at that particular truck stop. He had warned me not to smoke on the road. He made me promise I wouldn't smoke it until I got home. When I left him, I went into the truck stop and bought two cigars to dip into the bottle of embalming fluid mixed with PCP (wet) that I had just retrieved.

I just couldn't wait until I got home. Once I had the cigars in my hand it was like I was drawn to the bottle. My addiction got the best of me, and I smoked a cigar dipped in the wet. I pulled out of the truck stop and proceeded to drive back to Killeen. I don't know at what point I blacked out, but I did.. I blacked out, but I was still driving at 12 miles an hour on the busy highway.

I got arrested and don't even recall the arrest—that's how high I was. When I came to, I was in the ambulance, and the officer was holding my purse. I asked, "What happened? Did I kill anyone?" The police officer told me that I had hit his patrol car, but he was OK. He was very nice to me. The ambulance took me to the hospital to get blood work and to make sure I was medically fit for jail. After the checkup I was transported to jail.

I was released two days later on a $2,000 bond. When I retrieved my car from the pound, everything was scattered, and my bottle of wet was missing. I assumed the officer had taken it.

When Man got out of jail, she contacted me via Facebook right away. I responded, since I thought she was a good person. I was sure to find out what type of person she truly was. We hung out, got drugs, and each time she stole from me.

Mugshots from jail

Psych ward continued

Suicidal thoughts were a constant nightmare of mine. The feelings of loneliness, hopelessness, and emptiness always lingered in my head. But this time I was hallucinating. One particular day I called the police about a man standing on the front side of my house near the door. I could see his feet from the edge of my security camera. When the cops knocked on my door, I looked at my security camera, and I still saw the feet there. I wondered how that man could be foolish enough to still be standing there. I figured the cops had detained the man. So, I opened the door and the police proceeded to show me that the feet I supposedly saw were my water hoses lying in a bundle on the ground. I felt like such a fool for calling the police. But they were polite about it and went on their way.

A few days later I spotted the police across the street surrounding a house. There were three cop cars out there. I was peeking through my window when I thought I saw the truck that was parked in front of the house moving slowly. I thought, "Oh no,"—the man they were looking for was in this truck and was about to get a way. I ran outside with my phone and began recording the truck moving. When I saw a policeman come from the backyard of the house, I began to flag him down. When he glanced my way, I pointed at the truck and said he was in the floor of that truck. The police shined his flashlight inside that truck and all around it, even underneath, but didn't see anyone. The police officer began walking towards me, and I said I had the truck moving on my phone. When I proceeded to show it to him, two other cops walked up to me. As I was showing them the video on my phone, I realized the truck had not moved at all. They all looked at me strangely but didn't say much about the video. They were polite and said if I saw anything not to hesitate to call them. I said OK and closed my door. Once again, I was feeling out of control about the whole thing.

The next day I was sweeping, and I saw mouse poop all around the baseboard of my house. I also say mouse droppings in the cabinet near my kitchen sink. I was disgusted to think I had mice in the house. I ran and got my phone and called Orkin Pest Control and told them what I had seen. They said they had someone in the area who could come to my house and assess the matter. I was so happy that I could get service that same day. It was less than twenty minutes when the Orkin guy showed up. When he looked around the house and looked in the cabinet, he didn't see any mouse droppings. I was looking over his shoulders by now and was pointing the poop out to him. He politely but sternly said there was nothing there. I asked if he was sure and kneeled down beside him. And I saw for myself that there was nothing in the cabinet or around the baseboards. I told him that I was sorry for wasting his time. And he said no problem, but if I saw anything not to hesitate to call and he left.

I knew something was clearly wrong with me, and I made an appointment to talk to my psychiatrist. I informed him that I was feeling hopeless and that I was seeing things that weren't there. I explained what had happened with the police and Orkin a few days earlier. He suggested that I admit myself so I could get evaluated and get my medication adjusted if need be. So, I did just that.

I was admitted again to the psych ward. This time the patient-staff relationship was worse. The staff didn't seem to want to be there. They were lazy and slow to help with any of our needs, which was hard on us because we had to ask for everything. If we needed to bathe, we had to ask for soap, comb, toothbrush, and anything we needed. There was this patient who fought with staff for no reason. She would just snap in rage. I was so ready to get out of there. I got my act together quickly and lied to the doctor that I wasn't suicidal. I just wanted to leave because I feared for my life. I didn't feel safe. I knew I was safer in my own home. Plus, my medication had been tweaked, and I was feeling a little better at maintaining and fighting those suicidal thoughts.

DWI and jail continued

Seven days after my first DWI, I caught a second DWI charge, plus a felony charge. By this time, I was experimenting with various drugs like wet. When I was pulled over, I had a bottle of wet in my possession in a mini-Scope mouthwash bottle. I was too high to even know I was being arrested. I was jailed at McClennan County, Texas. They confiscated my bottle and sent it off for testing. And several days after my release from the second DWI, they came back and arrested me for possession of PCP.

On my first night in the McClennan County Jail, they assigned me to a top bunk. I was so uncomfortable and in too much pain in my back to climb up to the bunk. I was told by another inmate that in order to have a bottom bunk, you had to get consent from the doctor. I pressed the intercom to call the officer. Immediately the officer said they would inform the doctor. About an hour had passed and I hadn't seen the doctor. I pressed the intercom to call the officer again. I made my request again to see the doctor. The officer said to stay off her intercom. I pressed it again and again. But the officer ignored me. Next thing I knew, two officers came and told me that I was leaving and that they had a write-up in their hand. I was being thrown into segregation for disobeying an officer. Little did I know that segregation was a better place to be than in general population. It was a cell with its own toilet, one sink with a mirror, and a mat on a bunk. Also, in segregation, there was another inmate who was good at writing short stories, and that's how we passed the time away. She wanted to exchange info, but I had learned my lesson from Man, so I would change the subject all the time to avoid giving it to her. We looked forward to her writing every day. She wrote about romance, violence, etc. We also added some input to her writing to give her ideas on what to write about next. We looked forward to the different characters she would add as we gave her ideas of what we wanted to hear about.

While in jail I experienced a poor quality of food. They served mostly carbs and a small soggy salad with each meal, that I didn't eat. This food was harsh on my stomach and caused severe constipation. The mattress was not thick and caused severe body aches and stiff muscles. In addition, my full medication was not afforded to me, even though it was annotated in my VA medical records that I needed the full dosages. We were given one hour a day for recreation outside of segregation. That is when we could see male prisoners and where I met Tee. He was serving time for manslaughter and was waiting for his trial date. He had the biggest, most beautiful eyes, and we had good conversation. We would talk under the door whenever I was afforded recreation time. We got to know each other well and exchanged information so I could write him when I was released. He shared that fraternization was happening regularly between inmates and inmates with guards.

I was issued one towel, one washcloth, one sheet, one mattress, one uniform, one pair of underwear, one blanket, one hygiene pack with a spork, toothbrush, toothpaste, soap, comb, and one property box. Laundry days were Tuesdays and Fridays. We were given one hour out of our cells a day into the tank area. During that hour we would bathe, use the phone, watch TV, or talk up close to another "celly." That's when we would swap food or pass notes. In our cells we had a bed, toilet, sink, and a table. Because it was so cold, we made hats, shoes, and a pillow out of toilet tissue and water like a papier-mâché. I remained locked up in segregation for eight days.

Segration Tank Diagram

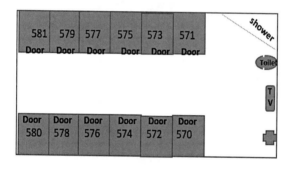

Cell Diagram

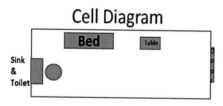

When I was released, my drug days were over. I had learned enough and experienced enough. They say you have to hit bottom before you are ready to stop using. The bottom for me was an unmanageable life. My life had spiraled out of control, and I had found myself in compromising position and places, dealing with untrustworthy people. I wondered how I had made it this far—how by some unwanted miracle my heart had not stopped. I knew I had to stop using. And these programs gave me a starting place for living a clean life, without drugs. Changing people, places, and things is the key to a successful recovery.

CHAPTER FIVE

RELAPSE

Did you know?

According to the National Institute on Drug Abuse, between 40 and 60 percent of people recovering from drug addiction relapse. These recurrence rates are similar to those of other chronic diseases, including Type 1 diabetes and hypertension (Advance Recovery System, n.d.).

Weight issues

My brickwork began restoring all the layers of my foundation, but as the masonry and mortar got weakened through the pressure of my desire to use, some bricks started to fall off again. Moving from D.C. to Texas wasn't what I had anticipated. I still couldn't hold a job down due to the pain or the symptoms from all the medication I was taking. The medication made me sleepy all the time, but it controlled my suicidal ideation. I had to take it, though, especially since two of my diagnoses were Major Depressive Disorder (MDD) and Borderline Personality Disorder (BPD). C. Elliott and L. Smith (2009) state that "BPD has nine major symptoms: impulsivity, self-harm, roller-coaster emotions, explosiveness, worries about abandonment, unclear and unstable self-concept, emptiness, up-and-down relationships, and dissociation." I had all of these symptoms. I also had symptoms that included hopelessness, helplessness, low motivation, anxiety, lack of energy, fatigue, and guilt. I questioned whether my brick wall could be restored, and whether I would be able to remain recovered from any mind-altering drugs or if I would fall back into a state of relapse. But I was willing to try this new way of living.

My single friends found hanging out at the same club week after week and seeing the same people pleasurable. The only thing we had in common by then was that we had all gone to Killeen High School. My relationships with my mother and daughter were very toxic at this point. Trying to resolve childhood resentments with my mom seemed hopeless. Either she would say to get over it or she would tell me that she didn't remember. One day the argument got so bad that she said she would just disappear out of my life. And she did just that. She stopped talking to me. When I would try to visit her, she would ignore me and pretend that she wasn't home. I believe my drug use had my feelings all over the place. Even my daughter, who was living with me, couldn't stand being there. And I couldn't stand her being there either. We would have physical fights all the time. What made it so bad is that my granddaughter witnessed us fighting. One day our physical fight got so bad that my daughter threw scissors towards me. I thought she meant to throw them at me, so I got them and ran towards her with a stabbing motion. She moved out that day, and she and my granddaughter moved in with my mom. Now they both were fed up with me. And I lost contact with them. If it weren't for my granddaughter going to school across the street from my house, I probably wouldn't have seen her either. But my granddaughter would come to my house after school until her mom got off work.

I was pretty much miserable with my whole existence. I indulged more and more in food just before I had the gastric bypass surgery. I thought after the surgery I was going to be happier and that my pain would be more bearable. But no, it made my psyche worse because now, after the surgery, I couldn't even soothe my depression with food. Although I tried many a day to eat at my old favorite buffets, my appetite had been altered. I had lost the desire to eat most foods, and my stomach got full after a few swallows, so I wasted my money going there. Between my previous drug use and my new inability to eat, I weighed 99 pounds. I was in a size two, the smallest I had ever been in my life. My head was the biggest thing on my body. My neck was sunken into my shoulders, and my collarbones protruded out. The little muscle and fat I once had was gone. You could see my bones sticking out all over my body. My hair was also falling out. I was a complete mess. While I was using, I didn't care about my physical appearance much. My every thought was on getting wet. My life had taken a turn for the worse. But you couldn't tell me anything. My saying at this time was that *I was living my best life*. But life didn't get any better.

When summer came, my daughter sent my granddaughter to go live with her father in Virginia. I was distraught. I was against my granddaughter going there since her dad hadn't been in her life much. But against my better judgment, my daughter sent her away. I had to bear this pain and my depression alone. Drugs seemed to be my only alternative to remove me from the sunken place

I found myself to be in. Whether it was opiates, weed, or wet, I didn't care. I just needed something to work. I was depressed and full of self-loathing. I thought about suicide every day. I often reflect that I was internally trying to kill myself. After all, I had tried in my younger years and been unsuccessful. I'd grown tired of living in excruciating pain. I just wanted out. I wanted relief. I had no one to talk to who understood what I was going through. I dared not tell my peer support counselor for fear I would end up back in the psych ward or rehab for a very long time.

This run with drugs and car wrecks resulted in a car being smashed up, insurance being dropped, DWIs, a felony charge, a surcharge, and attorney fees. I thought recovery was the answer. My probation officer mandated that I go to Narcotics Anonymous (NA) at least three times a week. And I was subject to random drug testing. By now my daughter had moved back in to help me out. The time away had made our relationship much better. We talked things through instead of fighting. She drove me to my NA meetings every week. With my daughter there, I dared not use again. So, I got back on track with my recovery. I had four months clean, and my daughter was proud of me. I was unsure recovery was what I wanted, but I just knew I had to do it. I was well on my way to a full life of recovery, or so I thought. They say you may have another relapse, but you don't know if you will have another recovery. I had been clean for four months when I went out with some friends and I had my usual glass or three of wine. The wine stirred up my craving for my drug of choice. I wanted wet again, so I was looking around the club and asking people who, from their appearance, seemed like they might know where I could obtain it. One of the people I asked went back and told my close male friend that I was asking for drugs. He came to me and said I was an embarrassment to him. That didn't sit too well with me, and it drew me into a deeper depression instantly. When I got home, I called a guy I had gotten cocaine from in the past. He didn't have wet, but he delivered me the cocaine and I used it. However, I was not satisfied because it wasn't the drug of my choice. It gave me a brain freeze. It felt as if I had drunk a frozen drink too quickly. I didn't like that feeling. So, I got my phone and went through all my contacts to find someone I thought had wet or knew where I could get it.

I found someone who did have wet and had them deliver it to me. I sat there looking at it for a long time, trying to decide if I was going to smoke it. Something inside of me was telling me no. So, I decided to throw it away. I knew if I threw it in my trash in the house it would be too tempting to retrieve it. I went outside and threw it in the outside trash. I was so proud of myself. Even though I did relapse with the cocaine, I was happy I could throw away the wet. I called my close male friend and told him that I had thrown it away, and he came over and got it out of the trash and took it from my property. That was a blessing in disguise because the next morning I went outside to the trash can and was looking for it. Now I was on my way to recovery again with four months down the drain.

There is a quote I like that says this: "I am not defined by my relapses, but by my decision to remain in recovery despite them."

According to M. Murdock's book, *The Uncommon Leader*, "Every man fails. Leaders simply get back up … and begin again." That's what I was determined to do. This relapse was not going to hold me down.

PART IIII

THE ROAD TO RECOVERY

CHAPTER SIX

....

RECOVERY

Did you know?

According to the National Institute on Drug Abuse, 85 percent of individuals relapse within a year of treatment; moreover, two-thirds of individuals return to drug use within weeks of beginning addiction treatment (Ashley Treatment, 2018).

REHAB

Inpatient Recovery

I entered the Women RISE (Women Recover in Supportive Environment) program. RISE is a recovery-based and trauma-informed intensive treatment approach tailored specifically for women veterans with a diagnosis of PTSD, mood or anxiety disorder, and/or substance abuse/dependence. I was clean for a total of three months my last time except for a one-day relapse. I stopped while I was in rehab. My three-layer foundation was being restored, and the trowel uniquely began to stack the bricks of my life back up again. This time the glue and water that formed the mortar restored my foundation. God put recovery within my reach. This was the starting point in my new recovery and in my abstinence from all mind-altering substances. Rehab entailed an eight-week program. The living arrangement was not enjoyable, with two people sharing a room with a full bathroom. Our room shared our bathroom with the only single-occupancy room next door. So, our room was the only room that had three people sharing a bathroom, unless you wanted to go to the bathroom in the hallway.

Women RISE programming is grounded in the highest level of evidence-based treatments, which are provided mostly in group therapy structured lessons that we had to attend all day. The lessons covered such topics as drugs, anger management, social skills, depression, stress management, dialectical behavior therapy (DBT) skills, occupational and recreation therapy, and more. I felt I was in school again, especially since we had to go to classes from 9 a.m. to 3:30 p.m. every day. The only downfall was that we lived with the same group of women we had to go to class all day with. It was challenging to be confined with the same group of women. Every so often a woman would get in a shouting match with another. People would get upset if a lady came to class late or if the same lady left the class early, claiming she had to go talk to her counselor. Seeing the doctor or your counselor was the only excuse we could use to miss class. They would send an instructor to come look for you if you did come up missing, so you had better be where you said you had to be. But I was learning how to manage my feelings and to deal with painful or difficult emotions, relationships, and situations more effectively. I was sure that these newfound skills would help me with my relationship with my mother and daughter. Any medication we did have to take was issued to us for a period of our time there until they felt we could manage taking it on our own. The program also gave me tools to help cope and manage my depression. If we went on a day or weekend pass, we would have to submit to a urine analysis upon our return. If we got caught with drugs in our system or if we didn't make it back before the door locked at 8 p.m., there were punishments handed out. One woman didn't make it in for curfew and they added an additional seven days to her stay, and she was banned from leaving the campus. Another woman failed her drug test and was restricted to the campus for the duration of her stay.

Abstinence from drugs was the help I needed to stop using. In the basic text it states, "Our track record shows that it is impossible for us to use successfully" (Narcotics Anonymous Fellowship, 2008). One thing they didn't teach was that we needed a support system and a sponsor to help us in those dark times that were sure to come. The trials of life will happen, but we must embrace our feelings and go through them. I learned that life happens, and the normal thing is not to use drugs to suppress our feelings, but to walk through the difficult period one day at a time.

Outpatient Recovery

One of the stipulations of my probation is to attend Narcotics Anonymous (NA) meetings. This is a group of recovering drug addicts helping each other to remain clean. The NA literature describes it as a program "for addicts who wish to pursue and maintain a drug-free lifestyle."

Anonymity is key to NA's success. Members understand and agree that what is said in meetings, as well as who they see there, remains at the meeting. But there was one problem. They wanted me to admit that I was an addict. I thought to myself, *I am not an addict.* I only did drugs off and on for three months. I wasn't like these people. I wasn't living under a bridge or anything like that. The thought of being an addict penetrated like a sharp knife. The reality was that I had been an addict most of my life, starting with sex and alcohol, then prescription pills, and then illicit drugs. What a miserable life I have lived as an addict in one form or another. I am an addict!

At my first NA meeting I didn't know what to expect. I pulled up to this all-beige brick building with the initials "NA" encased in a diamond shape written on the door. Later I came to realize that was the NA symbol. As I walked through the door, all eyes were on me. I felt so terrified. I quickly shuffled to a seat behind a big table that had people sitting around it. I was scared to make eye contact with anyone. I sat there listening to people one by one share their strengths, hopes, and experiences. There were people of all shapes and sizes. Some looked as if they hadn't had a place to stay in a while. I thought to myself, "I am not like these people." I figured I was just there because my probation officer said I had to be there three times a week and I needed my paper signed to prove I had attended the meeting. The longer I sat there listening, the more I realized that some of their experiences were just like mine. I, in fact, had something in common besides the drug use. When it came to my turn to introduce myself, I was hesitant to say, "I am Mattie, and I am an addict." But after I spoke, they told me they loved me and that they wanted me to keep coming back. And I did. I felt supported, and I saw other addicts staying clean and being OK with it. There were addicts ranging from four days clean to twenty-five years clean. I realized recovery was a lifelong process. I had a new title I recognized in my life. Yes, I am a recovering addict for life.

NA uses a primary text called the Basic Text. Members use this book as a guide for recovery along with the fellowship, experiences, and advice of other members. *Just for Today* states, "We use the Twelve Steps, and though they don't 'cure' our illness, they do begin to heal us" (Narcotics Anonymous World Services, 1991). In NA, we focus on learning the twelve steps.

The first step is to be abstinent from all mind-altering drugs, and to admit that I had a problem, that my life had become unmanageable, and that obsession, compulsion, and self-centeredness had been running my life. Addiction is a disease that was present long before I started using drugs, and to continue to use drugs would be insanity. We can't get well if we don't admit we are sick. I also learned that alcohol is a mind-altering drug that I had to stay away from. This step was easy for me to accomplish since I had already quit using in rehab.

The second step is to acknowledge that a higher power can restore me to sanity, because continuing to use would kill me, and through honesty, open-mindedness, and willingness, I would recover. I learned the values of spiritual principles such as surrender, humility, and service. Acknowledging I could not do recovery on my own was a turning point in my life. It was the eye-opening I needed to have.

The third step is to make a decision to turn my will and my life over to the care of God as I understand Him. There is a third-step prayer that says, "Take my will and my life. Guide me in my recovery. Show me how to live." The focus to surrender is the key. In this step I had to actually release my power to control my life. This was not an easy task, to let down my self-will. My ego said I could do this without God. But where had that gotten me? I had to release the desire to have control over people, places, and things.

The fourth step involves searching for and creating a fearless moral inventory of myself. I focused on my moral inventories—my liabilities and assets. I listed what is good about me and what is bad about me, getting to the nitty-gritty of why I act out. Creating this list was a hard task to do, seeing how my self-esteem was at an all-time low. But this step had to be done. Creating a list of the good, the bad, and the ugly helped me realize my strengths and weaknesses.

The fifth step is admitting to God, to myself, and to another human being the exact nature of my wrongs. This meant sharing my moral inventory with someone else, meaning admitting my wrongs to someone I trusted. Sharing our truths with someone can be embarrassing, but this is a sure way to build humility. I was told this is a necessary and big step in the recovery process. I utilized my sponsor as my listening ear for this step work. I trusted that she would keep my secrets, and this made it easier to confide in her.

The sixth step is when we are entirely ready to have God remove all these defects of character—the things we do when no one is watching. Are we really ready to pull out all of these weeds? Proverbs 3:5-6 says, "Trust in the Lord with all your heart and lean not on your own understanding; in all your ways submit to Him, and He will make your paths straight." God's inner surgery must be performed before we begin healing. The word of God cuts deeply, and His spirit can heal us. In the Bible it teaches that old things have passed away and all things have become new. This step was the preparatory command needed in my life. I was making the ultimate decision to give my faults to God—making an honest decision to turn my life over to my higher power.

In the seventh step, we humbly asked Him to remove our shortcomings. In the previous step we were ready to have God remove our character defects, and now in this step we must ask Him to help us with those shortcomings. This step requires action. I had to put my money where my mouth is and walk the talk. This step takes time because we don't change overnight.

The eighth step is when we make a list of all persons we have harmed and become willing to make amends to them all. I learned about writing an amends list and making a commitment to change from the harm I had bestowed on others. Seeking forgiveness has been key to my recovery. In making this list I realized that I myself was included in the people I had harmed. This self-evaluation helps me to not just see myself as a victim, but as a person who could overcome any obstacle that was placed in front of me.

The ninth step involves making direct amends to such people wherever possible, except when to do so would injure them or others. We must put the list from step eight into action and truly attempt to make amends with ourselves and others. Like step seven, this is an action step that requires us to actually go to the people we have harmed and try to make amends. One of the people I tried to make amends with was my mother. She was not ready to accept my apology, and it crushed me. But with this step I realized that everyone will not accept where you are in your recovery. All hope is not lost, and I have the strength to know that healing in others also takes time.

In the tenth step, we continue to take personal inventory, and when we are wrong, we promptly admit it. It is currently my daily walk to put away negative, hurtful actions, even if the hurtful action is to myself. In this step I learned that healing and restoration of our lives is an ongoing process. So, I must not give up hope, but trust the process. Things will work out in my favor if I faint not.

The eleventh step is seeking through prayer and meditation to improve our conscious contact with God as we understand Him, praying only for knowledge of His will for us and the power to carry that out. In this step I learned to put away self and rely on God to fight my battles. Praying and meditating are essential in this step. With the practice of the first three steps, this step becomes easier to do.

The twelfth step means that having had a spiritual awakening as the result of these steps, we try to carry this message to addicts and to practice these principles in all our affairs. Sharing our strengths, hope, and experiences with other addicts is a sure way to help the next person in their recovery process. I realized that reaching out to the next person is our ultimate goal in this recovery process. We also should repeat and apply these steps in all our affairs. The step work is a continual cycle in the rebuilding of my foundation.

As I worked the steps, I found out that I am a fractured individual. I have a long road to recovery, but it's possible. In NA I have been given a whole new way of life. I began putting the bricks back together in my foundation. Brick by brick and step by step is the only sane way to handle this recovery process—just one day at a time. *Living Clean* says, "Commitment to recovery is essential for us" (Narcotics Anonymous Fellowship, 2012). I didn't become an addict overnight, so recovery will not happen overnight.

On May 28, 2020, I had a burning desire to use. I chaired a meeting, and after the meeting someone asked me if I had any reservations. I said reservations about what? But as I thought about it, I had been thinking about using. Truth be told, if I believed my plug would give me what I wanted, I would have done it. If I knew my clean time wouldn't change,

I would use. If I knew there would be no embarrassment, I would use. However, drugs made my life unmanageable, and I wouldn't choose that for my life again. I have a year and six months clean at this time. I received my eighteen-month key tag. What an accomplishment that is. This journey is challenging. I heard someone at an NA meeting who was five years clean say she feels the same way, too. She said, "I did almost slip when I saw my old plug." This journey never ends. I must stick with my sponsor, do step work, and do service work. No, I don't have reservations, because I know that doing drugs is not an option for me. I was in a coma state; I got raped; I got robbed; I was put in jail; I was put in psych wards; I made poor decisions to drive under the influence; and I made a fool of myself. So, no, drugs are not an option. By any means.

There is a quote I like: "Recovery didn't open the gates of heaven and let me in. Recovery opened the gates of hell and let me out!" And that it did. I have never felt better about my life. I have hope again. I am in my right mind. I am learning the steps to making amends with myself and others. I am learning how to accept myself and the cards that I have been dealt. Accepting life on life's terms. Not running from my problems. Stopping the destructive behaviors that lead to jails, institutions, or death. Learning to do for others unconditionally. Not expecting anything in return.

Love is giving. I understand that my past is over. And I'm moving beyond the scars of yesterday and concentrating on my future. Murdock, 2006, states, "There is no Plan B for your life. There is only one plan … one Master Plan of the creator who made you. Consider nothing else as an option." I thank God that He didn't let me die in my active addiction.

CHAPTER SEVEN

SUPPORT SYSTEM, SPONSORSHIP, AND GOD:

I have a hard time feeling like I have the support of my family. I don't feel like I can talk to them about anything I am feeling or the urges that I may have. They just don't understand. I do know they wish me well, so that is all I can hope for. If I am going to have them accept me, I must accept them unconditionally. They, too, have been hurt by my addiction. I must remind myself of that and give them the patience to come around. As long as I stay clean, they have nothing to fear. I have everything to gain by being clean.

In the step workbook, it says that if the first step is about our "powerlessness over some other behavior that's made our lives unmanageable, we need to find a way to stop the behavior so that our surrender isn't clouded by continued acting out. Not every act of growth is motivated by pain; it may just be time to cycle through the steps again, thus beginning the next stage of our never-ending journey of recovery" (Narcotics Anonymous Fellowship, 2019)..

Living Clean says, "The message we carry has three parts: Any addict can stop using, lose the desire to use, and find a new way to live" (Narcotics Anonymous Fellowship, 2012).

It took about a year before I found my second sponsor. The qualities I liked in her were that she gave praise, and she was honest and real. She made me feel proud about my recovery. If I used, I would be embarrassed to see how my sponsor would feel about me. I would feel I let her and myself down. I would also let down the other members who have hope in my successful recovery. God helps us when we help others by sharing our experiences, hopes, and strengths. In September 2020, I marked eighteen months clean.

Support system, sponsorship, and God

Every day clean is a celebration. My brick and mortar were solid again, and the walls of my foundation are restored. Also, in 2020 my dad came to visit me just before the COVID-19 pandemic hit. He attended an NA meeting with me. After the meeting, when we arrived back at my home, he proceeded to let me know he was proud that I had found recovery—that he was honored to have experienced my NA meeting with me. And him saying that he loved me made me feel like that 12-year-old girl again. I welcomed my dad's opinion and praise. I was no longer living with the lack of the love from my father. I was no longer paranoid that someone was out to kill him or myself. I had several cameras installed around my house for that added peace of mind.

An NA sponsor is a member of NA, living our program of recovery, who is willing to build a special, supportive, one-on-one relationship with us. But as sponsees we must do the footwork to be successful in our recovery. My sponsor is such an added value to my life. A sponsor is someone to believe in me and in my recovery. She is a sponsor who has a sponsor who has a sponsor. What a blessing my current sponsor has been to me. They say the sponsor is the most important aspect to our recovery. Indeed, my sponsor is. She has blessed me by being available when I need to talk about an issue that is causing me anxiety. I recall one time when my dad was sent home on hospice, and how I dreaded that news. I was distraught because I lived in Texas and he lived in Virginia, and I didn't know if I would get to see him before he passed. I had a strong desire to use drugs, but I called her before I picked up a drug. She was able to soothe my mind and made me realize if I decided to use, I would be of no use to him. I knew she was right, and when I got off the phone, I began making plans to visit him. It was a successful trip. The Sponsorship pamphlet states, "A sponsor's role is not that of a legal advisor, a banker, a parent, a marriage counselor, social worker, or a therapist. A sponsor is simply another addict in recovery who is willing to share his or her journey through the Twelve Steps" (Narcotics Anonymous World Services, Inc., 2004).

When I have a setback, or I feel I want to use, I have someone experienced who can talk me off the edge. I must actively work with my sponsor about this desire to use. A sponsor is the key to gaining trust in other people. She shares her experience, strength, and hope. Because my sponsor is a recovering member, she shares a common bond of addiction and recovery. She can empathize with me. We need a sponsor to help us in our recovery. This is the therapeutic value of one addict helping another. My sponsor has helped me work the steps of my recovery. The Sponsorship pamphlet states, "Regardless of how we communicate with our sponsor, it is important that we be honest and that we listen with an open mind" (Narcotics Anonymous World Services, Inc., 2004).

Another aspect that has helped tremendously is going to psychotherapy counseling. When I began, I was meeting with a counselor every week. I met with a counselor to talk about how my week went and other matters that concerned me for that week. We'd discuss dealing with the relationship between my mother and me, or my daughter and me. We'd talk about my self-esteem and how I viewed my self-worth. We'd come up with new ways of looking at my life and the struggles I went through growing up. We'd discuss how I felt about trials of life on a daily basis, and how I handled the situation versus how I should have handled the situation. During COVID-19 my meetings happened online via Zoom. They are still as effective. Now I meet with the counselor every two weeks, but the format is still the same. The counselor assigns me various homework tasks to complete for the next week. Then when I come back the following week, we discuss the assignment and how successful or unsuccessful I have been in completing the task. My counselor and I have a good rapport, which is important for the effectiveness of the counseling session.

I also have my dad, who tells me all the time that he is proud of me. It feels good to hear that from him. I bubble up inside with joy like I am that 12-year-old little girl again. I am also grateful for my daughter who holds me down and takes me to my NA meetings. I am so grateful to still have my mother alive, even though our relationship isn't where I would like it to be. I am especially grateful for the pep talks my little grown granddaughter has with me. She is only 11 and has the wisdom of an adult. If I use, I lose. Lastly, I would be saddened for my loss of clean time.

"By staying clean, we begin to practice spiritual principles such as hope, surrender, acceptance, honesty, open-mindedness, willingness, faith, tolerance, patience, humility, unconditional love, sharing, and caring. As our recovery progresses, spiritual principles touch every area of our lives, because we simply try to live this program in the here and now" (Narcotics Anonymous Fellowship, 2008).

One of the recommendations from my sponsor was to write good-bye letters.

Good-bye letters

Good-Bye, Alcohol and Wine, May 2020

You cunning bastard, you tripped me up once and you tried to get me again and you succeeded. Well, I know I shouldn't cry over the loss of you, but I am. I hate you so much. You are a fake friend in my life, and you do not have my best interest at heart. So, what does that say about me? Why do I feel the need to want to be able to drink socially again? Maybe one day, but today that isn't a part of my recovery.

Good-Bye Wet, May 2020

It's been over a year since I've seen you, but I miss you. It's crazy after all you did to me and the places I ended up over you. You almost cost me my life several times. But I can't help thinking of the pain you relieve from my body while at the same time giving me so much energy and strength. You would black me out or cause me to numb all pain (neuropathy). There was one time you shut my body all the way down and I couldn't move. I was frozen so I couldn't go out. All I could do was lie there and go to sleep or die—lie there until you decided whichever outcome you were going to let happen. Another time you slapped my body around before knocking me out, and I woke up to find the rocker I was sitting in was on top of me. I was alone outside the front door of my house. Another time we went to jail together, but you left me to suffer the consequences. Another time you allowed me to get raped during the blackout you had me in. Other times you had me in a psych ward. I hate you for coming into my life. My life will never be the same because of you, or should I say because of me for letting you into my life. I did this to myself, so I have to live without you because I also almost lost my sanity behind you. Yes, you blacked me out, and I couldn't find my way in my own mind. I was looking for my eye socket. It was if my brain had twisted to the back of my head. I was frantic in restoring my sanity. But where were you during this episode? You left me alone again and again. How many times will I let you set me up, only to abandon me? No more.

CHAPTER EIGHT

LESSON LEARNED

Alcohol socially, today vs. future

One of the things I have learned is that I can't socially drink again. Smoking is a bad habit I picked up from using wet. You see, when I used wet, I would take a cigarette and dip it into the embalming fluid/PCP combo and smoke it. So, smoking has been a challenge to put down. Right now, I don't want to stop smoking cigarettes. But I will stop one day. Eventually I will conquer that, too. I have the hope in my God to help me.

Sex revelation

Through my course of running through men and being raped, I developed a lot of shame. The mere minutes of the sexual act are not worth the mental scars it puts on our hearts. "According to F. Jones' article, *"Love & Relationships: Talk like sex- Celibacy, Abstinence & Just saying no,"* "And there have been times when I allowed regret to take over as

I wished for the chance to turn back the hands of time and choose to abstain." Celibacy is the act of abstaining from sexual activity and, in most formal definitions, is almost always connected to religious or spiritual reasons. F. Jones also states that, "Some celibate people have had sex at least once, but now choose to wait until they are more comfortable with having sex again." Just saying no is what I choose for myself today. If God sees fit that I should marry again, this is when I will choose to unlock my celibacy. Narcotics Anonymous Fellowship 2012 states, "Being willing to see what has created our views on our own sexuality and the sexuality of others can help us to understand our beliefs." You see, the first command was given to Adam and Eve. Sex joins us spiritually, physically, and emotionally (soul ties). Consummating the marriage develops soul ties. The original intent was for the concept of one: Serve one God, one man with one woman, one marriage, one sex partner, one lifetime, one picture. Sex is good because sex was God's idea; however, sex was perverted by Satan. Satan came to break relationships. Sex is the only sin you sin against yourself.

Relationship revelation

"We need to trust before we begin to discern who is trustworthy. Discernment comes from hard experience: trusting people we shouldn't, being hurt, and coming back anyway" (Narcotics Anonymous Fellowship, 2012). After completing a self-inventory, I realized that self-isolation is one of my character defects that has cost me many friends. I don't mean to isolate, but I have been alone and had to survive alone all my life. That is all I know. But they say don't hang out with the last person you got high with by yourself. Because I could not accept myself, I expected others to reject me, too, if they really got to know me. That inner hatred of myself caused me to protect myself from vulnerability. I was rejecting others before they had a chance to reject me. Bottom line, I realized that with or without the approval of others. According to Narcotics Anonymous Fellowship in the 6th edition it states that, "I don't have to use old friends, places, and ideas are often a threat to our recovery. We need to change our playmates, playgrounds, and playthings."

Just For Today says, "We don't have to wait for an overdose or jail sentence to get help from Narcotics Anonymous" (Narcotics Anonymous World Services, 1991). And the basic text says, "Narcotics Anonymous is a fellowship of men and women who are learning to live without drugs. If the program worked for them, it would work for us" (Narcotics Anonymous Fellowship, 2008).

We can be addicted to anything that tastes good, feels good, or looks good. That addictive behavior is so cunning and baffling, manifesting in spending, shopping, and any other obsessive-compulsive act. I am an addict with addictive tendencies. I may have another relapse, but I don't know if I will have another recovery. Life is not guaranteed. But God wants us to have a fulfilled life. Life is a blessing from God, and we must cherish it. We must make a decision to treat others with kindness, with gentleness, and with the same concern we'd like to be shown. We all have a past, but thank God we have a future of eternal life. No longer do I have to endanger, humiliate, or abuse others and myself for the next fix. I have the self-acceptance that I am all right being an addict in recovery, that I am not perfect, but that I do have room to improve. If God is not enough, no person will ever be. Narcotics Anonymous Fellowship, 2012, states, "We come to understand that just being ourselves really is enough to be loved and cared for by others and by a power greater than ourselves."

HELPFUL SCRIPTURE

....

1 Corinthians 3:9: For we are God's fellow workers. You are God's field under cultivation, God's building. (NWT Study Bible)

Galatians 6:1: Brethren, if a man be overtaken in a fault, ye which are spiritual, restore such a one in the spirit of meekness; considering thyself, lest thou also be tempted. (KJV)

Galatians 6:10: As we have therefore opportunity, let us do good unto all *men*, especially unto them who are of the household of faith. (KJV)

Romans 1:11-12: For I am longing to see you, that I may impart some spiritual gift to you for you to be made firm; or, rather, that we may have an interchange of encouragement by one another's faith, both yours and mine. (NWT Study Bible)

1 Peter 4:10: As every man hath received the gift, even so minister the same one to another, as good stewards of the manifold grace of God. (KJV)

Proverbs 24:16: For the righteous one may fall seven times, and he will get up again, but the wicked will be made to stumble by calamity. (NWT Study Bible)

Matthew 6:33-34: But seek ye first the kingdom of God, and His righteousness; and all these things shall be added to you. Take therefore no thought for the morrow: for the morrow shall take thought for the things of itself. Sufficient unto the day is the evil thereof. (KJV)

II Corinthians 1:3-4: Praised be the God and Father of our Lord Jesus Christ, the Father of tender mercies and the God of all comfort, who comforts us in all our trials so that we may be able to comfort others in any sort of trial with the comfort that we receive from God. (NWT Study Bible)

SLOGANS

....

"One is too many and a thousand never enough."
"If you don't pick up, you won't get high."
"It gets better."
"Easy does it."
"No matter what."
"Dial 'em, don't file 'em."
"N.A., N.A.—Never Again, Never Alone."
"I've had a spiritual awakening."
"Don't count the days; make the days count."
"H.U.G.S.—Help Us Grow Spiritually"
"Meeting makers make it."
"F.E.A.R.—Face Everything and Recover."
"The masks have to go."
"Principles over personalities."
"Insanity is repeating the same mistakes and expecting different results."
"We are not responsible for our disease, but we are responsible for our recovery."
"H.O.W.—Honesty, Open-mindedness, and Willingness"

EPILOGUE
CONCLUSION

- I speak to those suffering from addictions to work, prescription medicine, sex, porn, alcohol, drugs, nicotine, caffeine, etc. No matter the many shapes your addiction manifests, staying clean and having sanity is your ultimate objective.
- Get to the root of your pain. In other words, what is your addiction masking? Only when you can answer this question can you have a successful path to recovery.
- We are in need of a personality change. The real problem lies in our thinking. NA works if you work it.
- Recovery is all about change. You can stop using, but can you not start using again? This will determine if you are addicted.
- Share my experience, strengths, and hopes with the addict who is still suffering.
- The only alternative to recovery is jails, institutions, dereliction, and death. So, choose life today.

BIBLIOGRAPHY

Advanced Recovery Systems. (n.d.) Recovery/
  Relapse/Triggers. Retrieved from https://
  www.drugrehab.com/recovery/triggers/
Ashley Treatment. (2018, May 27). Drug Addiction
  Recovery Statistics. Retrieved from https://www.ash-
  leytreatment.org/drug-addiction-recovery-statistics/
Cohen, I. Ph.D. (2018, July 13). How to Let
  Go of the Need for Approval. Retrieved
  from https://www.psychologytoday.com/
  us/blog/your-emotional-meter/201807/
  how-let-go-the-need-approval
Doheny K. (2011, November 23). Most Drug-
  Related Hospitalization. Retrieved from
  https://www.webmd.com/healthy-aging/
Elliott, C. Ph.D. & Smith, L. Ph.D. (2009). Borderline
  Personality Disorder FOR DUMMIES.
  Hoboken, NJ: Wiley Publishing, Inc.
Golstein & Orr (n.d.). Federal Drug Penalties.
  Retrieved from https://www.goldsteinhilley.
  com/drug-crimes/federal-drug-penalties/
Graves, J (2019, February 19). 17 Signs You
  Might Be a Workaholic. Retrieved from
  https://money.usnews.com/money/careers/
  slideshows/17-signs-you-might-be-a-workaholic

Heshmat, S. Ph.D. (2017, November 28). "7 Common Reasons Why People Use Drugs." Retrieved from https://www.psychologyto-day.com/us/blog/science-choice/201711/7-common-reasons-why-people-use-drugs

Jones, F. (2013, December 26). ""Love & Relationships: Talk Like Sex—Celibacy, Abstinence, & Just Saying No." Retrieved from https://www.ebony.com/love-relationships/celibacy-abstinence-and-just-saying-no-333/

Liades, C. MD. (2016, March 22. 8 Common Behavioral Addictions. Everyday Health Newsletter. Retrieved from https://www.everydayhealth.com/addiction-pictures/the-8-most-surprising-addictions.aspx

Murdock, M. (2006). The Uncommon Leader. Ft. Worth, TX: The Wisdom Center.

Narcotics Anonymous Fellowship. (2012). Living Clean: The Journey Continues. China. Narcotics Anonymous World Services, Inc.

Narcotics Anonymous Fellowship. (2008). Narcotics Anonymous 6th Edition-basic text. China. Narcotics Anonymous World Services, Inc.

Narcotics Anonymous Fellowship. (2019). The Narcotics Anonymous Step Working Guide. China.

Narcotics Anonymous World Services, Inc. (2004). IP No. 11 Sponsorship. Van Nuys, CA. Narcotics Anonymous World Services, Inc.

Narcotics Anonymous World Services, Inc. (1991). Just For Today – Daily Meditations for Recovering Addicts. China. Narcotics Anonymous World Services, Inc.

Owens P, Ph.D., Fingar, K, Ph.D. Heslin, K, Ph.D, Mutter, R., Ph.D, Booth, C., Ph.D. (2017, January). (H-CUP) Healthcare Cost and Utilization Project. Retrieved from https://www.hcup-us.ahrq.gov/reports/stat-briefs/sb220-Suicidal-Ideation-ED-Visits.pdf

Preiato, D (2020, May 4). 7 Harmful Effects of Overeating. Retrieved from https://www.healthline.com/nutrition/overeating-effects

Rawes, EJ (2014, September 20). Top 5 Money Problems Americans Face. Retrieved from https://www.usatoday.com/story/money/personalfinance/2014/09/20/wall-st-cheat-sheet-money-problems/15832929/

Rodriguez, T. (2016, September 26). 5 Things Every Woman Who Grew Up Without a Father Needs to Know. Retrieved from https://www.womansday.com/relationships/family-friends/q-and-a/a56444/fatherless-daughters/#:~:text=However%2C%20researchers%20have%20found%20that,with%20healthy%20relationships%20in%20adulthood.

SAVE. (2020, May 28). Suicide Facts: Global Statistics. Retrieved from https://save.org/

The Online Slang Dictionary. (2016, Apr 23). Retrieved from http://onlineslangdictionary.com/meaning-definition-of/lick#:~:text=verb,edited%20on%20Apr%2023%202016.

ACKNOWLEDGMENTS

I am eternally grateful to my daughter, Shanetta, for being the grounding source through times my anxiety wanted to take over. Thank you, James, the person who encouraged me to write the memoir on my experiences. Thank you, Charlene, for being the example that I could write and publish a book. Thanks to my granddaughter, A 'Lisa, the gem of my eye, a glorious distraction in my earlier days of my recovery. I thank everyone immensely for the love, prayers, and support.

ABOUT THE AUTHOR

Marianela Leonard rose through the ranks of the U.S. Army to Sergeant First Class, SFC, E-7 before retiring after twenty years. During her last five years in the military, she worked in the White House Situation Room. She earned a B.A. in Information System Management (IFSM) and an MBA from National-Louis University (NLU) in Illinois. Marianela is a resident of Killeen, Texas. She is a daughter, mother, grandmother, and entrepreneur. When she is not writing, you can find her doing service work at Narcotics Anonymous (NA) or binge sharing on Zoom NA meetings, walking her dogs, enjoying her backyard oasis, and making gift baskets and jewelry.